A special gift for

____

With love

____

Date

____

Our purpose at Howard Books is to:

- *Increase faith* in the hearts of growing Christians
- *Inspire holiness* in the lives of believers
- *Instill hope* in the hearts of struggling people everywhere

Because He's coming again!

Published by Howard Books, a division of Simon & Schuster, Inc.
1230 Avenue of the Americas, New York, NY 10020
www.howardpublishing.com

10 Digit ISBN: 1-58229-569-7; 13 Digit ISBN: 978-1-58229-569-5
10 Digit ISBN: 1-4165-4158-6; 13 Digit ISBN: 978-1-4165-4158-5

10 9 8 7 6 5 4 3 2 1

Manufactured in the United States of America

For information regarding special discounts for bulk purchases, please contact Simon & Schuster Special Sales at 1-800-456-6798 or business@simonandschuster.com.

Personalized scriptures by LeAnn Weiss, owner of Encouragement Company
3006 Brandywine Dr., Orlando, FL 32806; 407-898-4410

Hugs for Friends
Interior design by LinDee Loveland
Edited by Philis Boultinghouse

Hugs for Friends, Book 2
Edited by Between the Lines
Interior design by Stephanie Denney

Big hugs™ for Friends

Stories, Sayings, and Scriptures to Encourage and Inspire

G. A. Myers
and LeAnn Weiss
Personalized scriptures by
LeAnn Weiss

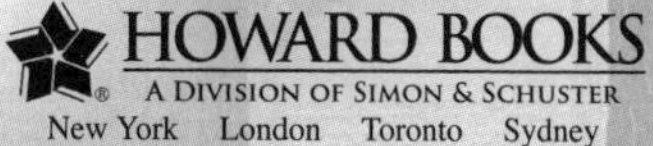

HOWARD BOOKS
A Division of Simon & Schuster
New York London Toronto Sydney

Stories, Sayings, and Scriptures to Encourage and Inspire

hugs™ for friends

Stories and Personalized Scriptures by
LEANN WEISS

Messages by
CARON LOVELESS

Contents

one
steadfast friend 1

two
forever friend 17

three
any-weather friend 35

four
empathetic friend 55

five
joyful friend 73

six
selfless friend 87

seven
faithful friend 105

A friend is the hope of the heart.

—Ralph Waldo Emerson

one

steadfast friend

Catch a glimpse
of my *incredible* love for you!

I pray that you, being rooted and established
in love, may have the power to grasp
how **wide**

and *long*

and high

and deep is my completely

unconditional love for you—

a *love* that surpasses all human knowledge.

My forever love, *Jesus*

—from Ephesians 3:17–19

Friends possess remarkable keys. They open the locked doors of our lives. They give us entrance to places we'd never dare go by ourselves. They fling wide the gates of lush, secret gardens. They take us to treasure rooms glistening with gifts we're sure we don't deserve.

Friends unlatch the windows of our souls. They grip the drapes we've drawn around ourselves and yank them back to let God's gleaming light stream in. They pull and tug until the windows pop open and fresh, new breezes fill our musty hearts.

When storms throw trees across our path, a friend will lend her strength to haul the logs away. Friends are not fazed by our roadblocks. They come equipped with chain saws. They help us chop our obstacles like firewood then strike a match to them.

inspirational message

They make sparks fly up from the flames. They say, "Why not sit awhile and warm yourself by this nice fire?" When the smoke clears, friends pass out coat hangers and feast with us on roasted marshmallows until the last ember dies.

Friends have sight where we are blind. They are guides through the jungles of our past. They are fearless to face the dangers we know lurk beneath the brush. Friends hack and slash at the wild, clinging thoughts that bind us. With grace, they loose us from our blindfolds then tie them on branches, marking a trail for the future.

Friends create breakthroughs. The best ones are agents of God. Like him, they stand us in front of a mirror and introduce us to ourselves.

A genuine friendship is a heavenly present. It blesses our hearts because God's love is in it.

—Evelyn McCurdy

More than anything else,
Nancy yearned to be *loved*.

A Hug for Nancy

"Welcome to The Logan," Joyce chirped as she raised her head from her paperwork to greet her new guests. "We're glad you've chosen to spend some time with us."

Joyce and Larry Coffin owned and operated a quaint home-style hotel near the boardwalk in Ocean City, New Jersey. At first glance, the two young women standing on the other side of the check-in counter seemed fairly typical of their summer vacationers. Both were in their early twenties, and they had come to The Logan for some relaxation and sun.

But as Joyce gave them their room keys and the standard instructions, she noticed that one of the young women, Nancy, kept her head down and eyes to the floor, obviously avoiding eye contact. She didn't speak a word but left all the

talking to her companion. Uncomfortable with Nancy's glaring silence, Joyce was relieved when the two women departed for their room.

The next morning when Nancy came through the reception area, Joyce smiled warmly as she offered a morning greeting. "Hi, Nancy! How are you this morning?"

Nancy returned her greeting with stark silence.

Maybe Nancy hadn't heard her. She tried again, "Did you sleep well?"

Still no response.

Undaunted, Joyce made another effort, "You must have slept well because you look so bright-eyed and bushy-tailed!"

Joyce's cheerful words were met with more awkward silence. Not knowing what else to say, Joyce was relieved when Nancy's friend appeared and rescued Joyce from her fumbling monologue. The two women headed for a day on the beach, and Joyce returned to her duties.

Over the next few days, Joyce made a deliberate effort to converse with Nancy. Although Nancy never spoke a word, a weak smile or uneasy giggle would occasionally escape her lips. It seemed as if she wanted to let Joyce in but didn't dare.

Something about Nancy pulled at Joyce's heart. Why had Nancy built such a barrier between herself and the rest of the world? What had caused her to retreat into silence?

Soon it was time for the two unlikely friends to check out and return to their homes in Pennsylvania. As they walked out of the hotel, Joyce felt an urgent need to do something to break through Nancy's self-imposed shell. Running up to her room, Joyce frantically searched for some token she could give Nancy. As she looked around her room, she silently prayed, *Lord, is there something I can give Nancy to let her know you love her?*

Finding a small gift, Joyce hurriedly wrapped it and ran outside, hoping it wasn't too late. She breathed a sigh of relief when she spotted the two women loading their things into Nancy's 1978 Buick Skylark.

"Wait, Nancy! I have something for you. I just wanted you to know that you are special and that God loves you. I'm glad you came." As Joyce handed Nancy the trinket, she felt compelled to accompany it with a big hug. As she wrapped her arms around her shy, perplexing guest, Joyce felt as if she were hugging a lifeless mannequin.

Nancy was obviously taken off guard by the hug but maintained her unresponsive exterior as she abruptly and

silently retreated into her car. As the car left the loading area, Joyce prayed, *Lord, I feel so helpless and frustrated. I tried to show her your love, but I failed. I so wanted to hug her hurt away, but I was naive to think I could make a difference with such an insignificant gesture. You know what makes Nancy hurt and what will heal her. I'll never see her again, but you can be with her always. Please wrap your arms of love around her and keep her in your care.*

Several times during the months that followed, Joyce felt prompted to lift Nancy's unknown hurts to her all-knowing heavenly Father. Her prayers were often accompanied by a longing to decipher the riddle of Nancy's silence.

Meanwhile, back in Pennsylvania, the effects of that one "insignificant" hug were beginning to bear fruit. Joyce's persistent kindness and simple hug sparked a major turning point in Nancy's life. A peek back into Nancy's childhood reveals why Nancy had shrouded herself in silence.

Nancy had grown up in what she considered a fairly typical Pennsylvania Dutch home. But Nancy's home lacked even the most basic displays of affection, and her parents strictly limited her social interaction. One of five children, Nancy never had a birthday cake or party. She wasn't allowed to participate in extra-curricular activities or go to slumber parties or have friends over to her house, and she couldn't date until after high school graduation. Nancy's parents took her and her siblings to church when she was young, but they eventually stopped going; Nancy and her sister occasionally went on their own. Nancy did have a few pleasant childhood memories of family vacations and exchanging gifts on Christmas morning, and she knew her parents hadn't neglected her emotional well-being intentionally; but the lack of affectionate expression from her mom and dad had deeply wounded her heart.

Her dreams of friendship had been dashed on several occasions when she'd dared to open her heart—only to find rejection. Lately, she had managed to maintain a couple of shallow friendships, but those activity-driven relationships left her hungry for more. She longed for someone who dared look beneath the surface. She wanted more than a companion for movies or shopping. She wanted someone she could trust with her pain.

More than anything else, Nancy yearned to be *loved*.

By the time Nancy checked in to The Logan, she was emotionally crippled. Fearing further rejection, Nancy had padlocked her heart and withdrawn into the safety of an almost silent existence. She spoke only when necessary to

the few people she allowed inside her lonely, walled fortress. When Joyce had tried to penetrate her refuge with kindness, Nancy hadn't known how to respond.

But as Nancy thought back to Joyce's kindness and her surprising hug two months earlier, something warm began to stir in her heart. Not allowing herself to debate, she opened her desk drawer, took out a paper and pen, and began to write.

> Dear Joyce,
>
> You may not remember me. I'm the lady who didn't talk. I loved my time at your hotel this summer. You had no way of knowing it, but you gave me a very special "gift." Your hug was the first I ever remember receiving in my whole life.
>
> I know that God loves me and that I need to get close to him again. Thanks for letting him love me through you.
>
> I will never forget.
>
> Love,
> Nancy

As soon as Nancy put down her pen, the inner debate began. She was so afraid of appearing a fool and of being rejected once again. But something deep inside insisted that

Joyce would make a trustworthy friend. As Nancy sealed and mailed the letter, she hoped against hope that Joyce hadn't given up on her and would write back.

Several days later, as Joyce shuffled through a large stack of mail, she came across a letter that had been forwarded from The Logan to their winter home in Maryland. She puzzled over the unfamiliar name and address as she slit the envelope open.

As Joyce read Nancy's brief letter, tears streamed down her cheeks. Her receptive heart was quick to pick up on the tentative plea for friendship written clearly between the lines. Joyce responded immediately, and a special, long-term friendship was born.

Future trips to Ocean City were always spent with Joyce at The Logan, and over time, the warm, caring woman trapped inside Nancy was set free. Reminded of God's love through the embrace of Joyce's arms, Nancy slowly learned to trust again. Through the years Nancy and Joyce have continued to exchange letters written on "hugs" stationery. Several times a year they talk on the phone. They frequently exchange little "hugs" gifts, and they faithfully remember each other in their prayers.

Today, almost twenty-five years after that first hug,

Nancy is a totally transformed person. It's as if someone gave her a heart transplant. She enjoys chatting on the phone, is active in ministry, and looks forward to graduating from Bible school. Nancy is now so outgoing that she even talks, shares, and prays with perfect strangers. And when she visits her seventy-three-year-old mother, she expresses her love with an extra big hug.

"Never in a million years would I have suspected that God would use such a small effort on my part to bring about such big results," Joyce reflects. Joyce has no doubt that it was actually God who hugged Nancy that summer day in front of The Logan. He simply borrowed her arms.

two

forever friend

Love as I have unconditionally loved you.

I demonstrated the very essence of true friendship when I *willingly* laid down my life for you.

What blessings I have waiting for you.

Think about it—

I'm living *within you!*
I've reconciled you to my Father!

Now, you can enjoy a wonderfully exciting friendship with the Most High God through me —forever!

Love,

Your *Messiah and Friend*

—from John 15:12–13; Romans 8:11; Romans 5:10–11

We've heard how the heat of battle can take mere soldiers and turn them into soul mates. Somehow, the fire of affliction fuses a bond between those who might, under "normal conditions," overlook or even avoid each other.

It seems the strongest and most enduring friendships are not necessarily the oldest ones. They're often those forged in the furnace of adversity. Maybe this happens because emergencies heighten our senses and, at the same time, make us vulnerable. Tough challenges reduce our reserve. They disarm our defenses. They ripen our hearts for relationship and lay our souls open to intimacy.

Sometimes, we're so wounded that we'll take help from anyone. Like a drowning victim, we thrash and choke and beg for air. Then, out of nowhere, comes a hand. At that moment,

inspirational message

we don't care whose hand it is or where it's been. It's all we've got, so we grab it. And once we're on land and breathing again, we shake that hand until our arm falls off. That hand was our hope. And a relationship blooms from a rescue.

Crisis breeds camaraderie. It turns total strangers into cherished confidants. We're relieved to discover someone whose experience bears a striking resemblance to our own. It gladdens us to know we're not alone. We will always enjoy our childhood friends—the ones we lived next door to or met on the playground in second grade. But when we grow up, our needs change and God provides friends of a different kind—friends who are formed in the School of Hard Knocks, companions who've come from the classroom of life.

Some people come into our lives and quickly go. . . . Some stay for awhile and leave footprints on our hearts, and we are never the same.

—Unknown

Helen discovered the secret
that we are only able to love
others because God first loved us.

Unlikely Friends

The first meeting of Mrs. Helen Correa and Mrs. Lillian Allen was anything but friendly. Their husbands, Mac Correa and Joe Allen, both worked at WYCO Tool Company in the Chicago area. The two wives met for the first time at the annual company holiday dinner in 1949. As Mac Correa scanned the festive room full of fellow employees and their spouses, he was surprised to spot the Allens. "Hey, honey, look; that's Joe and his wife—the couple I told you about," Mac whispered as he pointed across the room to identify the Allens. "Remember, they're the couple whose six-year-old diabetic daughter just died." He briefly recounted the tragic story of how a medical intern, in a rush to leave for a Christmas party, had accidentally administered a fatal overdose of insulin to the Allens' little girl.

On the other side of the room, Mrs. Allen felt like a fish out of water in the jolly holiday atmosphere. *Why did God take our precious Carrie?* she silently asked for the thousandth time as she tried to maintain her composure. *How can all these people be so happy when my world has just fallen apart?* She tried to pretend she was listening to the meaningless babble that surrounded her. Everyone was talking about their families and the festive gatherings they'd had on Christmas day. Each mention sent a stabbing pain through her already shattered heart. And then there were the empty efforts at condolences. She knew they meant well, but none of these people knew her or her pain. No one knew what to say, yet everyone felt they needed to say something. The resulting comments were stilted and awkward—anything but comforting. She hadn't wanted to come tonight, but several friends had insisted that it would be good for her to get out since she had been cooped up in the house with her other four children since Carrie's burial the previous week.

Mrs. Correa observed Mrs. Allen from a distance. *What is she doing out in public so soon? Her poor little daughter was just buried on December 23rd. How inappropriate for her to be here for a holiday celebration.* As she scrutinized Mrs. Allen's behavior from across the room, the sympathy and compassion Helen had felt when she first heard of their tragedy drained from her heart. She was absolutely appalled when she caught Mrs. Allen cracking a half-smile a few times throughout the evening. *How could a loving mother smile so soon after losing a child?* Mrs. Correa was unquestionably confident that she would never smile again if she lost her child. *And she is supposed to be such a religious woman. Mac said she was downright fanatical! What kind of religion would let a mother be out partying at a time like this?*

Meanwhile, Mrs. Allen's first impressions of Mrs. Correa were reciprocally negative. In her eyes, Mrs. Correa was nothing but a "harsh-looking, overpowering, heavily painted, cigarette-smoking, worldly feminist."

When they were formally introduced later that evening, the interaction was extremely awkward. Trapped by civilities, neither of them could hide their disdain. Both were relieved at the conclusion of their brief encounter. Quite obviously, they had absolutely nothing in common. Even more convinced that the Allens were "religious extremists," the Correas made it a point not to have anything to do with them outside the necessary contact between the husbands on the job.

But in April of 1953, the Correas' world crumbled. Their four-year-old son and only child, Jerry, lost his life to an incurable kidney disease.

When Joe Allen told his wife of the tragedy and suggested they go to the wake in West Chicago, Mrs. Allen felt as if she'd been hit by a truck. The news stirred up painful emotions, and the thought of seeing another young child in a tiny-sized coffin was almost more than she could bear. But, like her husband, Mrs. Allen knew in her heart that it was the right thing to do.

When Mrs. Correa saw the Allens, she flashed back to their only meeting over three years ago at the Christmas dinner. Mrs. Correa now recounted Mrs. Allen's smile in a different light. Overcome with grief she hopelessly cried out, "Mrs. Allen, how did you ever live through the experience of losing your daughter?"

Mrs. Allen softly replied, "It was only with God's help that I was able to survive."

About a week after Jerry's burial, Mrs. Correa was surprised to receive a letter from Mrs. Allen inviting her to lunch. Even though she was desperately hurting and in need of comfort, she wanted nothing to do with this religious fanatic and the glib panaceas she might offer. As she considered how to turn down the invitation politely, another piece of paper tucked inside the envelope caught her eye. She hesitantly unfolded the beautiful stationery and began to read . . .

He is a little flower
　　plucked from this world of woe.
He will blossom in God's garden,
　　and by his love will grow.
Left from the evil of this world,
　　his life shall perfect be,
Dwelling in the mansions all through eternity.

Oft times our hearts are troubled,
　　and oft we wonder why
Our little ones from heaven
　　must leave our homes and die.
And yet we cannot think of them as dead—
　　but just away,
For they are with our blessed Lord
　　forever more to stay.

So when your heart is heavy
　　and sorrows bend you low,

In the secret of His presence,
    you'll find the heavenly glow.
He will give new strength for every day
    and all our sorrows share.
So weep not loved ones for him;
    he's in our Savior's care.

The beautiful poem had obviously been written by Mrs. Allen after Carrie's death. It had been modified for Mrs. Correa's son, Jerry. Tears welled up in her eyes as she read the tender words of hope, and when she had finished reading, a little door in her heart opened—just a bit. *Anyone who could write a poem like this after her child died must have something special.* Grief-stricken, lonely, hopeless, and without direction, she decided to accept Mrs. Allen's invitation and find out if she had any help to offer her. *My life is meaningless; if Mrs. Allen turns up empty, I will be no worse off than I already am.* When Jerry died, Mrs. Correa's whole world had died with him; this was the first glimmer of hope she had felt.

When Mrs. Correa arrived for lunch, she saw that the table had been painstakingly set, as if it were being featured in *Good Housekeeping Magazine*. Mrs. Allen's care showed in every detail—from her dress, to her hair, to the fine china, to the flowers in the vase, to the colorful presentation of the table and the scrumptious food. The extra effort caught Mrs. Correa off guard.

But Mrs. Correa was pulled back to reality when her hostess sweetly asked, "Would you mind if we thanked God for the food?"

Of course she minded. *There she goes again with her religious mumbo-jumbo*, she thought as she quickly located the two exits out of the house. *Still*, she reasoned, *it is a lovely meal, and I don't want to appear ungrateful.* So she kept her annoyance to herself and bowed her head.

They hadn't even gotten to dessert when Mrs. Allen purposefully reached behind the server and picked up a Bible. "Would you mind if we read the Bible together?" Without waiting for a response, she opened the book and began reading passages about heaven. Mrs. Correa's anxiety was growing by the minute. *This is going too far. This religious woman is out of control!* But as Mrs. Allen read from the Bible in her lap, her voice was so full of hope and assurance, that Mrs. Correa was enthralled.

> For we know that if the earthly house of our tabernacle be dissolved, we have a building from God, a

> house not made with hands, eternal in the heavens. (2 Cor. 5:1 ASV)
>
> For our citizenship is in heaven; whence also we wait for a Savior, the Lord Jesus Christ. (Phil. 3:20 ASV)
>
> But according to his promise, we look for new heavens and a new earth, wherein dwelleth righteousness. (2 Pet. 3:13 ASV)

Mrs. Correa had never thought much about heaven before. But she knew the Bible was a special book, and if it said there was such a place, she now realized that Jerry must be there. Relief flooded her heart as she imagined her precious Jerry safe in the arms of Jesus.

Mrs. Allen stopped reading and caringly looked up, establishing clear eye contact with Mrs. Correa as she said, "One day Jesus is coming back to take all of those who believe in him to be with him forever." She lovingly but boldly confronted, "Will he take you?"

Caught off guard, Mrs. Correa defensively sputtered, "Well, I've attended Sunday school since I was three . . . I've taught Sunday school for years . . . I even sing in the church choir!" But as she added to the list, she could tell Mrs. Allen didn't seem at all impressed with her deeds.

Mrs. Allen continued reading, now from John 5:24, "Verily, verily, I say to you, He that heareth my word, and believeth him that sent me, hath eternal life, and cometh not into judgment, but hath passed out of death into life." As Mrs. Correa listened to this verse, she realized for the first time that Jesus was the only acceptable substitute for her sin. Nothing else mattered.

That afternoon of April 21, 1953, Mrs. Correa received the most important hug of her life when she invited Jesus to become her savior and best friend. This new friendship with Jesus would now eternally transform all other relationships, as it is the very basis of love.

Mrs. Allen now became Lillian and a dear friend to Helen Correa. Helen discovered the secret that we are only able to love others because God first loved us. He calls for us to examine all of our relationships through his eyes of unconditional love.

Today, almost fifty years later, my grandmother, Lillian Allen, and Helen Correa share a lasting friendship. Although separated by more than three thousand miles,

they've discovered that "a lifetime is not too long to live as friends." Through the years, Helen Correa has enthusiastically shared her testimony at Christian Women's Clubs, groups, and with everyone she meets. As a result of the hug of salvation that my grandma shared with her, Helen's husband, Mac; their entire family; and many others have come to know Jesus Christ as their best friend too.

"I thank God that your grandma saw my need and cared enough about my eternal destination to get involved in my life and lead me to an eternal friendship with Jesus Christ," Helen gratefully shared with me. "Because of him, your grandma and I are forever friends!"

And thanks to their best friend, Jesus, they both look forward to continuing their friendship in heaven and to their upcoming reunion with Carrie, Jerry, Grandpa Joe Allen, my mom, and many other forever friends who have already gone ahead.

As Michael W. Smith sings, "Friends are friends forever if the Lord is the lord of them."

three

any-weather friend

I've chosen you!
You are *holy* and *loved*.

May you consistently live your life with
a heart of compassion,
daily demonstrating *kindness*,
humility,
gentleness, and patience.

Choose to gracefully *forgive others* when
they disappoint you or hurt you—

just as my Son, Jesus, forgave you.

Most importantly, let love be the superglue that bonds all your relationships and friendships.

Love,

Your *God of Love and Forgiveness*

—from Colossians 3:12–14

One of the best things about having a good friend is all the grace you get. You just sit around being you, and a good friend makes you think she wouldn't dream of having it any other way.

For instance, you can have a rotten attitude and end up saying things you're sorry for later, and a good friend will hardly be fazed by it. She'll act like it's no big deal. She'll just put her arm around you and say, "Don't worry about it. Everyone has a bad day now and then"—even if you've had ten bad days in a row.

And a good friend isn't surprised by your mistakes. She expects them. Somewhere, fairly early in the relationship, a good friend will find out the truth

inspirational message

about you. She'll witness your weaknesses firsthand. And it's at this point that your friend, if she's really a good friend, will decide to stick by you anyway. Oh, in the early days she may have whined and complained a bit about your less than desirable traits, but before long, something grows in her and outweighs them—it's called *grace*. Then, instead of fussing about your ten-thousandth tardiness, she just plans for it. She brings a book or buys a paper or files her nails. And when you finally come racing up, out of breath, with a million and one excuses, she looks at you, smiles, and says, "Don't worry about it. Really. It's okay. I haven't been waiting that long."

The face of a friend reflects God's grace.

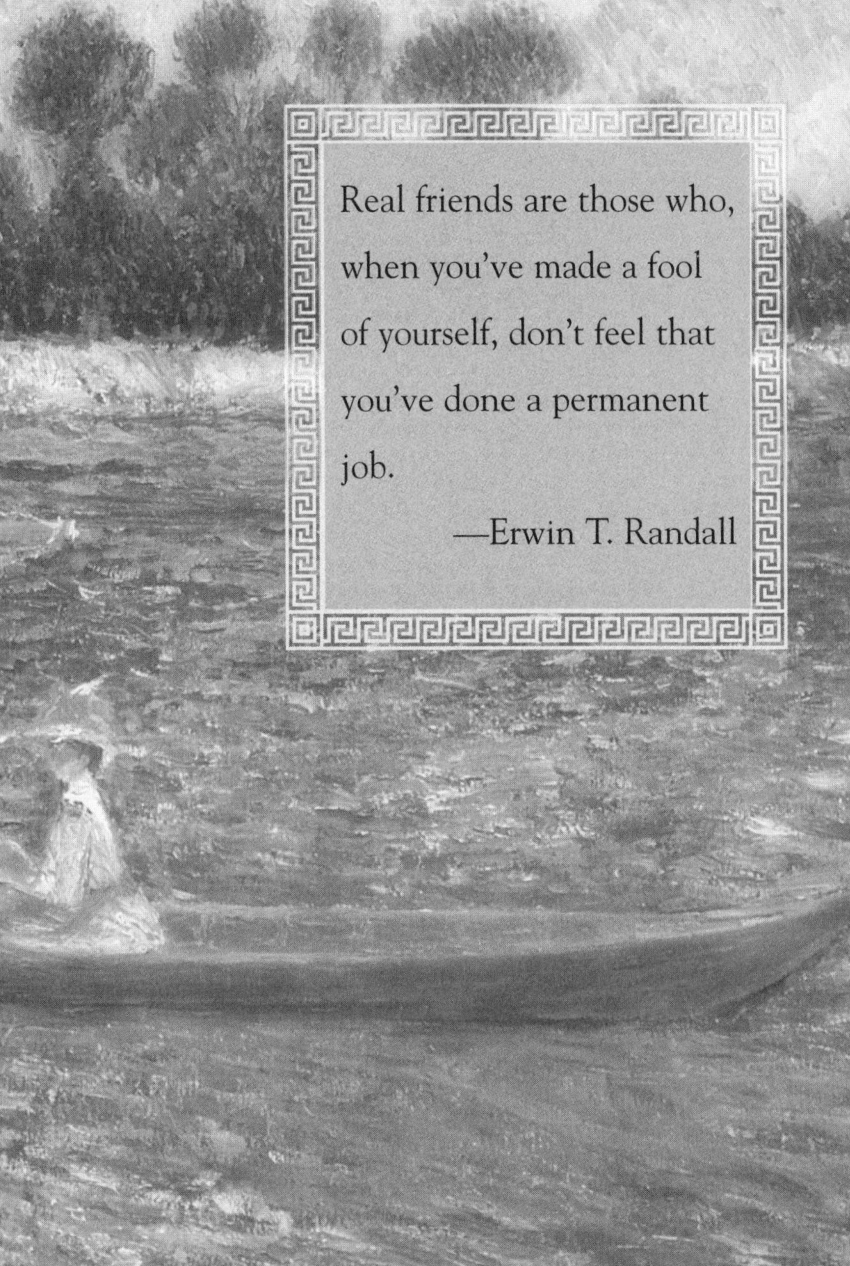

Real friends are those who, when you've made a fool of yourself, don't feel that you've done a permanent job.

—Erwin T. Randall

Despite all my shortcomings
and humdinger flub-ups,
my friends still loved me.

Forgiven Fiasco

"Come with us, Sue," I cajoled. Sue and I were close friends, prayer companions, and tennis partners. Sue's idea of camping is a comfortable room at the Hilton. You know—hot showers, soft beds, air conditioning, and swimming pools.

Sue *might* have felt okay about camping at a well-lit, just-off-the-freeway, security-patrolled campsite with flushable toilets and paved roads. But a canoe trip to a remote clearing in the forest was way beyond her comfort zone. No electricity or running water, the open forest for a rest room, snakes, mosquitoes—it was all too much. But after much cajoling and negotiating, Sue reluctantly agreed to go. "It will be a fun adventure you won't forget," I firmly reassured her.

The night before our Friday departure, I stayed up almost all night packing. My motto in traveling is "Why leave the

kitchen sink? It might come in handy." I like to anticipate problems and be prepared. But all my preparation was undercut when one of my friends (cheered on by my sister and another friend) decided at the last minute to become a self-appointed inspector and rifled through my backpack and bags, removing three-quarters of my "important stuff." My objections were to no avail, and we departed with a much lighter load.

In protest, I defiantly vowed not to speak on the drive to the forest. It didn't help my already challenged attitude that the three co-conspirators enthusiastically responded, "Do you promise?"

We finally arrived and quickly loaded the canoes. Just shortly before sunset, we pushed off from Katie's Landing. Sue, my cousin Jamey, and I were in the first canoe. I was designated navigator of our canoe since I was the only one in it who had made this trip before. My sister Pat, Terri, and Don (all of whom had been with me on our previous trip) were in the second canoe. Having a highly competitive nature and still a little incensed about having to leave my emergency supplies behind, I raced ahead of the other canoe.

Less than an hour into our trip, we had lost all daylight. Our canoe was still in a substantial lead. Occasionally, we would pause and wait a few minutes in hopes that the other canoe would catch up. I wasn't thrilled about our breaks, but I agreed, since the breaks gave me the perfect opportunity to set off some of the smoke bombs I had hidden in my pocket. They created a magnificent visual effect—trails of colored smoke streaming down the river in the moonlight. Those snapping alligators didn't know what to think.

Despite our stops, the other canoe was nowhere in sight. But we continued on, confident that they would soon reappear. "How much farther is it? Are you sure you know where you are going?" Jamey asked.

"Don't worry, we can't miss it!" I assured them. "You see, the last time we canoed to this campsite at night we thought we would never find it. But then, we came to the well-lit ranger station. This nice ranger told us that our campsite was only a half-hour away on the left side." I continued, "So all we have to do is wait for the ranger station and paddle on for another half-hour . . . piece of cake!"

We continued our fast pace without a trace of the second canoe or the ranger station. After what seemed hours, my cousin excitedly reported that he saw the ranger station in

the far distance. Later, he updated us, "Hey, I see a bridge coming up!" Knowing there were no bridges along our route, I was convinced he was seeing a mirage. I must admit that I was very puzzled when we passed under a bridge.

Later, Sue said she saw the light too. Finally, I saw the light. It was getting brighter and brighter. Soon the entire right side of the bank lit up. We were at a marina—not at all where we intended to be. We found a small restaurant, and having only four quarters between us, we seriously contemplated volunteering to wash dishes in exchange for a warm meal. Unfortunately, the kitchen had already shut down. We were surprised to learn that it was already past midnight.

By talking with some of the locals, we learned that we had drastically overshot our campsite by several miles. Assessing the situation, we further discovered that our canoe had all of the sleeping bags while our friends in the second canoe were carrying all of the food and tents. Worried that they would be cold without sleeping bags, we decided to backtrack and try to find them.

This time we had to paddle against a strong current. It was outright chilly for Florida residents. The temperature dropped almost 40 degrees that night. All of that stuff I was forced to leave behind would have come in real handy.

We came to a fork in the river and had to make a choice. Should we go right or should we go left? We went right—not sure at all that we had made the correct choice, but we had to keep moving or we'd never find our way. As we paddled along, the foliage became quite thick—like in one of those creepy, foggy scenes in movies shot in the Florida Everglades. Barely able to see a foot ahead, we were guided only by the dim light of our flashlight and the eerie glow of the moon shining through the trees.

Because I was sitting in the front of the canoe, my face was the first thing to collide with a massive spider web that bridged the width of the river. A few seconds later, I let out a death-defying shriek when a gargantuan spider crawled up my arm and neck and across my face. His legs were long and hairy and nearly spanned my entire face. Ugh!

"Look on the bright side . . . at least it wasn't a water moccasin," I tried to comfort my crew. Big mistake. From their horrified reactions, I realized that they hadn't been thinking about the possibility of uninvited poisonous snakes slithering from the overhanging branches into our craft. Until now.

To our dismay, the river path we had chosen got narrower and narrower and finally ended. We had to turn around and make our way back to the main river. Jamey and Sue finally decided enough was enough. Sensing a potential mutiny, I followed their demands and guided us to the side of the river. Securing our ship to a tree, we set up emergency camp.

Jamey conducted a snake and wild animal check. At first, we were thrilled to find my pup tent in the canoe. But, it didn't help because the stakes were in the other canoe. On the bright side, we were able to get a fire started with my two remaining smoke bombs, and we had *all* the sleeping bags. However, we would have gladly traded the sleeping bags for the tents and the food. We split a single beef jerky and a smuggled candy bar.

Exhausted from hours of canoeing against the current, the three of us just lay there motionless under the stars. Every so often someone would pipe up, "What was that?" or "Did you hear that?" in response to the multiplied sounds of the forest.

About an hour after we stopped, we heard a large rustling noise moving through the forest. Crackling leaves. Snapping twigs. Stammering, Sue asked, "A-a-re there b-bears in these parts of F-Florida?" as we prepared to run for our lives.

Much to our surprise, Pat, Don, and Terri emerged from behind the trees guided by the smoke from our fire. "Where in the world have you guys been? We searched for you for hours last night. We had given you up for alligator bait!"

"LeAnn was playing with smoke bombs and must have missed the ranger station," my cousin tattled. Our three friends looked puzzled.

"It's a long story . . . I must have missed the ranger station while I was setting off the smoke bombs. We ended up at some marina and had to turn around," I sheepishly confessed.

"What ranger station?" Don asked.

"What do you mean 'what ranger station?'" I replied. "You were all on the last trip. Remember, after canoeing in the dark for what seemed like an eternity, we finally saw the light of the ranger station on the right," I recounted.

I concluded by their still puzzled looks that they had had some kind of a twilight-zone experience stripping them of their memory. I continued in an effort to jolt them back to reality. "Remember, the nice ranger was sipping coffee by his fire? He told us our campsite was about a half-hour down the

river on our left. *Now* do you remember?" I frustratingly asked, still wondering how they could totally forget such an important detail.

Pat, Don, and Terri broke into hilarious laughter. "What in the world is so funny?" I impatiently inquired.

"You were looking for a ranger station?" Don questioned, laughing even louder.

"Now we know you're blind!" my sister added.

Much to my dismay, they insisted that there never was a ranger station or a ranger. My "ranger station," they said, was a tent pitched in the forest at the right side of the river. And my "ranger" was just an ordinary camper. (Unfortunately for me, he wasn't there this weekend.)

"They're just pulling my leg to get back for all of the practical jokes I've played on them," I said, still totally convinced I hadn't imagined my ranger. After we loaded up our sleeping bags and put out the fire, we headed for our designated camping site. It turns out, we were only about a half-hour short of our real camp site.

Shortly after we arrived, it started pouring. In fact, contrary to the predicted weather report of a sunny weekend, it poured all day. Everyone had nothing to do except rehearse the fiasco I had single-handedly created.

I was bombarded with complaints and subjected to hours of interrogation, like "How in the world could you have mistaken that tent for a ranger station?" Every detail of the scenario was examined and magnified under a microscope. Complaints of soreness from the ten extra hours of paddling and exhaustion from no sleep were laid at my feet.

I'd finally had enough of their harassment and laughter and slipped out of the tent unnoticed. Death by pneumonia would be better than this kind of razzing, I decided as I sat sulking in the rain. It took them about an hour to realize that I was missing.

Sue and my sister Pat snuck up behind me. "Hey, where have you been? Come back to the tent with us; you'll catch a cold out here," one of them said.

"It's all my fault! I'm sorry I ruined everyone's weekend. I'll just stay out here," I pitifully sniffled. Sue and Pat embraced my cold, rain-drenched body. "Hey, we're sorry for giving you such a hard time. It's okay. It was an honest mistake," said my sister.

"Yea, just think of the adventure we would have missed if you weren't along," Sue chimed. "Your friendship adds so much spice to my life," she said as she hugged me again. When we went back to the tent, they wrapped a nice

warm blanket around me and handed me a cup of hot chocolate.

Unfortunately, however, Murphy's Law remained in effect for the rest of the weekend. I was in charge of washing the pots and pans, but it was dark and I was afraid of water moccasins down at the river, so I decided I would just put the lids on the pans and wash them in the morning. In the middle of the night, we heard loud, clamoring noises. We were under attack! It turned out to be a gang of hungry raccoons that took off with our pots and pans. Also, I somehow managed to lose a borrowed, two-hundred-dollar sleeping bag.

But I learned a valuable lesson about friendship that weekend. Despite all my shortcomings and humdinger flub-ups, my friends still loved me. But, the most important thing I learned was the truth of 1 Peter 4:8 that love and friendship truly cover a multitude of faults and differences. Isn't it freeing to know that we don't have to be perfect?

Today, when we tell the story of our adventurous camping trip we roar in laughter. And the story gets better and better each time we tell it.

P.S. After we finally returned to civilization, I contacted the other campers from the previous expedition who all verified that there was no ranger station. I was sentenced to a life of wearing glasses and contacts following a comprehensive eye exam. However, to this day, I still suspect a conspiracy. I'm tempted to retrace our journey in daylight in search of my ranger station, but we've never gone back.

four

empathetic friend

Prayer summons Me!

Where two or more of you come together in my name, *I am* there with you.

The prayers of a righteous woman are powerful and *effective*.

Seek me eagerly and you *will* find me!

Love,

Your *Heavenly Father*

—from Matthew 18:20;
James 5:16; 2 Chronicles 15:15

Right away, from the very first week, God seemed to know that the world would be too wild and wooly for us to make it on our own. He looked at Adam's single self and announced: "It's not good for man to be alone." Then he went to work and fashioned a friend for him named Eve.

When Noah came along and the rain became a flood, God knew Noah would be going through some pretty rough waters. So, he sealed Noah up in the ark and brought his family along for the ride.

God gave Joshua to Moses as a companion for his journey through the wilderness. For forty years they walked and talked and checked their maps, until finally they found the Promised Land.

inspirational message

Daughter-in-law Ruth was God's gift to Naomi after the rest of her family had died.

In young David's most desperate hour, the Lord found Jonathan to be exactly the kind of friend David needed to make it to safety.

When everyone and everything was ripped from Job's hands, God allowed the comments of Job's comrades to keep him company.

And even as his only Son traveled dusty roads and sailed stormy seas, God flanked Jesus with faithful friends and followers.

The Father knew we couldn't make it on our own either. So he birthed us into families. But he doesn't stop there. Once we've been born again, he sets us up with a loving community that laughs with us and cries with us and prays us on to forever.

To live in prayer together
is to walk in love together.
—Margaret Moore Jacobs

The three friends clung to
each other and to the Lord
as their uncertainties escalated.

Shared Pain

January 31, 1993, seemed an ordinary night in the small Kuna village of Pucuro, Panama. That quiet Sunday evening was hot and muggy, and Tania and Mark Rich were relaxing in their hammocks in their living room, each cuddling one of their small children.

Although she'd only been in Pucuro a short six months, Tania, a third generation missionary, felt right at home in the jungle. Nancy and Dave Mankins and Patti and Rick Tenenoff—their co-missionaries—had been invaluable in helping Tania and Mark learn the Kuna language and culture.

Tania finally got up from her cozy hammock to put the baby to bed. After eleven-month-old Jessica was in the crib, Tania realized it was beginning to get dark. Living in a

village without running water or electricity, she decided to tackle the pile of dinner dishes and put the laundry away while there was still some light.

As she worked, something nagged at Tania, telling her she needed to put Tamra to bed too. But she had so much to do, and there was so little light left. Hurrying through her chores, the persistent feeling that she needed to get Tamra from Mark's hammock intensified.

Finally, Tania gave in and put the dish she was washing back in the sink. She walked into the living room, scooped her tired two-year-old into her arms, carried her to the bedroom she shared with her younger sister, and tucked her in bed for the night. Just as she kissed Tamra's cheek, she heard a loud commotion outside.

Tania's thirteen-year-old Kuna helper ran to the front door to see where the noise was coming from. But before she could open the door, three men in dark clothes and bandanna masks burst through the door, touting machine guns and yelling orders in Spanish. "Sit down on the floor! Put your hands up!"

Still in the room with her young daughters, Tania could only hear what was going on. Petrified, her heart stopped

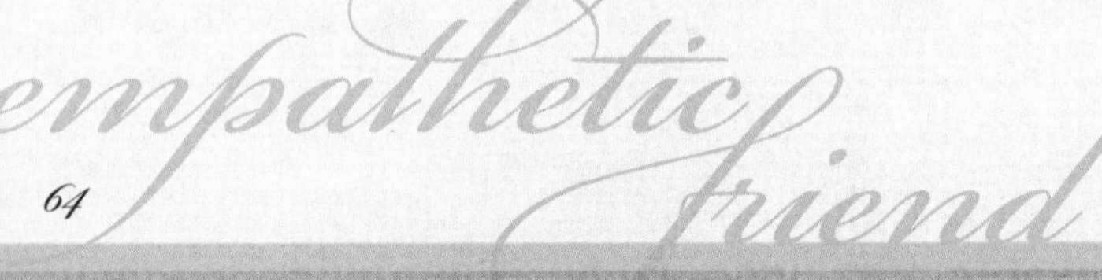

when she heard a gun shot followed by dead silence. Paralyzed with fear, frantic thoughts raced through her mind. *Have they killed Mark? Are they going to kill me and my children?* She wanted to run for help, but there was no escape—and even if there was, she couldn't leave her children. She began to earnestly pray in Spanish.

Tania heard footsteps throughout the house. The sound of water squishing in boots told her that these strangers have come from across the river. They were talking in Spanish rather than the Kuna dialect. "Señora, Señora," Tania could hear a man calling as he searched for her. She wanted to slip out of the bedroom so he wouldn't see the girls, but she was frozen with fear.

When the flashlight shined into the girls' room, Tania finally mustered the courage to say, "Here I am, what do you want?" They conversed in Spanish, and he instructed, "Give me your money . . . all of your money."

As Tania left the girls' bedroom with the man, she glanced across the kitchen into the living room and saw her husband lying face down on the floor with his hands tied behind his back. Mark started to struggle when he saw the man heading toward their bedroom with his wife.

Tania was relieved to know that her husband was still alive.

"It's okay, honey, they haven't touched me," Tania reassured him in English. At her words, Mark settled down.

Tania carefully followed all their orders. When they asked for sugar, she even volunteered a bag for them to carry it in. Then, as they instructed, she quickly packed a suitcase for Mark. Miraculously, Tamra and Jessica slept peacefully throughout the entire ordeal.

The sound of more gunfire rang out from across the village, and Tania knew that the Mankinses and the Tenenoffs had been invaded as well.

Just a few hours later, the three missionary wives sat huddled around Patti Tenenoff's kitchen table. Tania's two daughters and Patti's three children were asleep in a back room. According to village sources, all three husbands had been taken across the river on a trail leading to Columbia. The women and children were unharmed and together, but they were dazed and afraid.

The Kuna village where they were stationed was a small village of three hundred people in the middle of the rain forest. There was no police or military help. No telephones, no 911 emergency system. The captors had taken their only radio, which was their sole link to the outside world. Their mission plane wasn't scheduled to come for several more days, and they feared that the guerrillas might return to seize the plane if they waited. They were all alone—except for God and each other.

Acutely aware of their isolation from the rest of the world, they turned to God. "Lord, we need to know what to do. Please wake up people around the world and lead them to pray for us."

As the three frightened women prayed together, they felt a supernatural peace. Calmness and direction filled their hearts. They knew God was with them and that people were praying.

The only way out of the village was by canoe—and it definitely wasn't safe to maneuver the river by night. Nancy took charge: "I feel our husbands would want us to leave first thing in the morning." Tania and Patti agreed.

The three wives wearily bunked down for bed in the wee hours of the morning at Patti's house. After a fitful few hours of sleep, the women and children awoke early and prepared for the uncertain journey ahead.

Guarded by a Kuna man at each end of the canoe, the disoriented passengers left their homes with heavy spirits and headed down river to the next town. Tania, her two

daughters and her Kuna helper, Patti and her three children, and Nancy sat in the crowded dug-out canoe, praying that God would intervene. Three hours later, they disembarked at another village. Here, they finally communicated with their sponsors, who promised to have an airplane waiting for them at the next village. The weary travelers reluctantly piled back into the canoe for another strenuous four-hour trip to meet the plane that New Tribes Mission was sending to rescue them.

When they finally reached their destination at 5:30 that evening, they were exhausted and spent, but relieved to find a Cessna plane waiting for them as promised. As the airplane took off and the three friends watched the jungle disappear below them, reality hit. They could no longer hold back the tears. They sat together, sobbing and holding each other, feeling guilty for "abandoning" their husbands and afraid for their lives. *Would they ever return to their homes and the Kuna friends they had grown to love?* The future loomed ominously.

In the following days they learned that New Tribes Mission had received a call from F.A.R.C., a guerrilla group in Columbia, claiming responsibility and demanding five million dollars in ransom for their husbands' release. The women knew that the mission couldn't pay the ransom without jeopardizing the lives of thousands of missionaries around the country. *How would the revolutionaries react when their demands weren't met? Were their husbands safe? Had they been fed?* The three friends clung to each other and to the Lord as their uncertainties escalated. All the while, the growing prayer support of people around the world surrounded and comforted them.

Leaving Panama without their children's fathers to return to the States was another tumultuous emotional cornerstone. But Tania, Nancy, and Patti held each other up and shared the strength of the Lord.

In the six long years since witnessing their husbands being forcefully dragged off into the jungle, Tania, Nancy, and Patti have experienced every gamut of feeling from faith, to frustration, to anger, to confusion, to despair, and then to hope again. They've been separated from their husbands for much of their married lives.

Mark Rich missed seeing his daughter Jessica's first steps and both of his daughters' first days of school. Imagine the sadness Tania felt when little Jessica innocently volunteered, "Mommy, I would give away all my toys, even Cubby [her favorite teddy bear], if it would bring Daddy back."

Both of Nancy Mankins's children, Sarah and Chad—who were living in the states at the time of the kidnapping—have married while their dad has been held hostage. Everyone prayed up to the day of each wedding that Dave would get back to give his blessing.

Patti's young son, Lee, offered to go live with the guerrillas so he could be with his daddy again. Nancy and Tania have supported Patti as she's asked the question David asked in the Psalms, "Why so long, Lord, why so long?"

During all the pain and heartache, the three women have grown to lean on each other as friends. Like no one else, they truly understand the gut-wrenching emotions each other faces on a daily basis. Each of them has experienced the peaks and valleys of faith as life continues without their husbands.

Together, they help each other through the painful birthdays, anniversaries, holidays, and everyday reminders of the men they love and dearly miss as their nightmare continues. The three friends have traveled around the world together, meeting with queens and presidents, petitioning for their husbands' releases. When Tania broke into tears, overwhelmed after another media interview, Nancy and Patti were by her side to encourage her.

empathetic friend

Wherever Mark, Dave, and Rick are being held, their wives are comforted by the belief that their husbands are supporting and encouraging each other too.

Every morning Tania cries out to God, "Help me to go through this day joyfully, no matter what happens." During these long years of waiting together, the friendships of Tania, Nancy, Patti, and their children have been strengthened by the vast circle of friends around the world who lift them up to the Father every day in prayer. And they welcome new friends, like you, who will pray for their husbands' safety and return as well as for their children who desperately want their daddies to come home.

UPDATE: While there hasn't been any direct radio contact from the guerrillas since January of 1994, the Columbian guerrilla organization F.A.R.C. has claimed that Mark Rich, Dave Mankins, and Rick Tenenoff are still alive as recently as September of 1997. Tania, Nancy, and Patti request your prayers for wisdom and energy for the New Tribes Mission hostage crisis team, which has spent thousands of tireless hours trying to reunite their families.

Internet users can visit www.ntm.org for periodical updates and prayer suggestions.

five

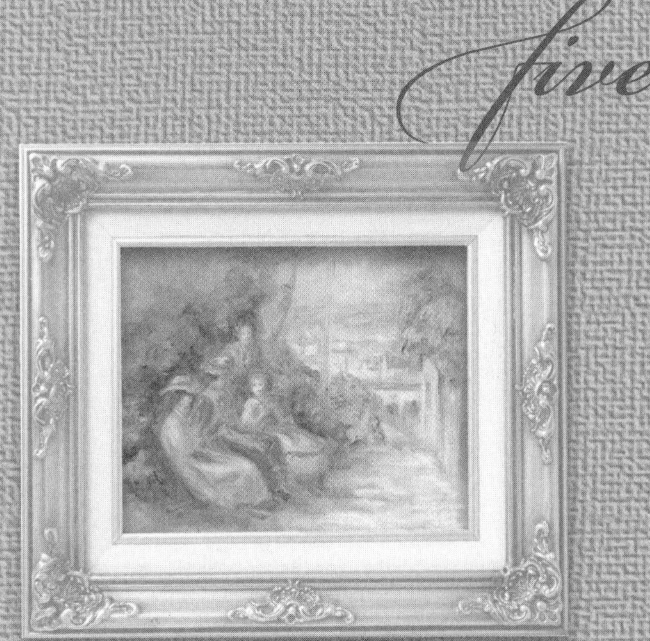

joyful friend

Look for my splashes of *joy*.

Laughter is good medicine—it's a great "shock absorber" for life's unexpected bumps. It helps take the monotony out of everyday life.

Don't miss out on the continual feast of a *cheerful* heart.

You'll see that a happy heart bubbles over into a smile.

And it's *contagious*!

Love,

Your *God of Joy*

—from Proverbs 17:22; 15:13–15

F—a *friend* never *fails* to be *faithful*, even when others *falter*. She won't say, "You're *fat*," (even if you are) or *focus* on your *flaws*. She is the *first* to point out your *finest features*. A *friend* will *fortify* your *fragile frame*. She will *free* you to *flourish*. A *friend* will never *forsake* you.

R—a friend is a *rare* and *ready rock* you can *run* to in the *rain*. She will *rescue* you from *rushing rivers—regardless*. She will *revive* your heart, *refresh* your soul, and *reassure* you of *rapid recovery*.

I—a friend is not *impatient* or *impolite*. She will *inquire* about your day and *include* you in her plans. She will *identify* your most *incredible ideas* and *ingenious innovations*. A friend is *interesting*, *inspiring*, and *indispensable*. She is the keeper of your most *intimate* secrets.

inspirational message

E—a friend is a friend till the *end*. She is *eager* to listen and *easy* to talk with. She's your most *energetic encourager*. A friend will *embrace* you *even* in the midst of your most *embarrassing encounters*.

N—a friend will *not nag* (unless it is absolutely *necessary*). *Naturally*, she knows your deepest *needs* and is also *nice* enough to *nudge* you when you're *neglecting* your *nest*, being too *nosy*, or contemplating *nonsense*.

D—a friend is *devoted* and *dependable*. Her *destiny* is to *divert* you from *defeat*, and her *devices* for *depression* usually involve the *delicious*. It's a friend's *divine duty* to *drown* your *disappointments* and *dispose* of your *dismay*, and many times she *does* it in a most *delightful* way!

Laughter is the language of the young at heart. And you know what? You don't have to be happy to laugh. You become happy because you laugh.

—Barbara Johnson

A boring, seemingly wasted day was transformed into a treasured memory by the laughter of friends.

Garage Sale Escapades

Faced with an empty nest after her three grown boys had flown the coop, Pat sold her spacious 2,500-square-foot Laguna Miguel home and purchased a condo.

Preparing for the big move, Pat realized that over the past seventeen years, she had accumulated a house full of *stuff*. Since moving into her new condo meant losing 1,000 square feet, Pat had to choose between downsizing and wall-to-wall, floor-to-ceiling boxes. Pat opted for a garage sale.

After countless hours of sorting and tagging a lifetime of memories, the big day arrived. The garage was filled with a collection of bargains—appliances, books, records, knick-knacks of every imaginable variety, things her boys no longer wanted, and an assortment of odds and ends.

Huge signs were posted and a tantalizing ad sure to

attract bargain hunters had been placed in the local newspaper. With the help of her good friend, author and speaker Marilyn Meberg, Pat was armed and ready for the anticipated frenzy of garage-sale addicts. Everything had to go. Pat was eager to sell and prepared to make price-cutting deals to assure that her accumulated loot was hauled away. Pat and Marilyn eagerly took their stations and waited for the customers to pour in.

But Pat had forgotten to take one minor detail into account—the weather. California had been experiencing a heat wave, and this particular Saturday turned out to be the record-breaking day. The thermometer soared to a sweltering 103 degrees. If they had cracked eggs in the miscellaneous pots and pans they were trying to sell, the heat would have fried them.

Pat and Marilyn watched as one by one, cars began to approach the driveway, slow down, and pause. Occasionally, they could even see noses pressed against the air-conditioned windows as passengers carefully examined the wares, focusing and pointing at items of interest. But as the two women watched in dismay, each car drove off without actually stopping to ask prices or make a deal. Soon, the

"Warning—I brake for garage sales" bumper stickers would drive out of sight.

What a disaster! The sizzling heat was converting die-hard garage-sale junkies into drive-by shoppers. Pat and Marilyn sat in the sweltering heat of the garage, using garage-sale treasures as makeshift fans and guzzling frigid liquids in hopes of avoiding dehydration or sun stroke. Old LP records melted and warped in the sauna-like conditions, and colorful books faded under the intense glare of the sun.

In a valiant effort to divert their attention from the blistering heat, they rummaged through the discarded items looking for launch pads onto memory lane. "Remember when you gave in and bought this for the boys?" Marilyn asked as she picked up an old skateboard.

Pat grimaced as she held out an old pair of bell-bottom jeans. "Can you believe these are actually coming back in style?"

"Remember when we were on that health food fad and you bought this yogurt maker?" Marilyn chuckled.

By early afternoon, only one customer had braved the heat to examine their goods. Dripping with sweat and bored to tears, the two friends were still reminiscing over historic

tokens when Pat spotted the old trombone case—a relic from her past. To Marilyn's amazement, Pat picked up the trombone and started blowing.

"Gosh, how long has it been since you played that thing?" Marilyn chaffed in response to the out-of-tune but recognizable song. "I didn't realize you'd ever had lessons."

Out of breath, Pat took a short break to explain that her musical career had started in the second grade. Because her seven-year-old arms had been too short to reach the trombone slide, she used to kick it with her foot. Marilyn laughed as Pat recalled how she had once missed the slide and accidently kicked the music stand off the stage and into the audience during a recital. "It's probably been a good twenty-five years since I've played."

"Hey! Can you play 'When the Saints Go Marching In'?" Marilyn asked. Rising to the challenge, Pat was determined to oblige her friend to the best of her rusty abilities. Although the gritty trombone slide hadn't been oiled in decades, Pat belted out the tune with enthusiasm. Suddenly, the dismal day was transformed into a slap-happy, giddy party as Marilyn began to march around the garage to the beat of the song, arms flailing dramatically as she conducted an imaginary band. Pat energetically joined the march, and the two long-time friends pranced around the garage without a care as to what passersby might think.

Soon, the jocular ruckus began to attract attention. One of Pat's sons emerged from the icy air-conditioned house to see what all the commotion was about, but he quickly buried his face in his hands as he observed his mom and Marilyn laughing and cavorting around the garage with the old trombone. His chagrin only served to energize and encourage their slap-stick performance.

Carloads of people actually began to stop to see what all the excitement was about. Some even joined in the escapade with requests of their own. "What about 'Dixie Land'?" "Do you know how to play 'Daisy, Daisy'?" As Pat whole-heartedly tooted away, Marilyn, whose special laughter has earned her a reputation, laughed so raucously that tears were streaming down her face.

Everyone seemed rejuvenated by the jovial mood, in spite of the intense heat. One carload of passersby turned out to be a group of friends Pat hadn't seen in years, and they enjoyed a surprise reunion.

But despite the crowds their revelry drew, Pat and Marilyn barely made enough sales to cover the cost of the ad in the paper. One of the few items that did sell was her dad's

set of old golf clubs, and she learned too late—just as she sold them for a "song"—that the set was a valuable antique. She ended up donating almost everything to charity, except the sentimental old trombone, which she decided she just couldn't part with. But the two weary women were still chuckling when the Salvation Army truck pulled away with a truckload of "priceless treasures." A boring, seemingly wasted day was transformed into a treasured memory by the laughter of friends.

Life is full of unplanned detours, less-than-desirable situations, and downright failures; but we can gain the upper hand if we'll latch on to a friend who can help us hurdle the obstacles of discouragement and defeat. So let your hair down a little and loosen up. Leap into the joyful journey God has tailor-made just for you. As my friend Barbara Johnson says, "The key is learning to look for the splashes of joy in the cesspools of life!"

six

selfless friend

I never intended for you to be a lone ranger. You were *designed* for relationship.

A **friend** increases your yield, helping you reach the potential I've destined for you.

When you **fall**, your friend is right there to help you up.

Pity the person who doesn't have anyone to **stand** with her in hard times.

But a three-cord strand with me at the center is not easily **broken**. Not even during earth-shaking, life-and-death trials.

Love,

Emmanuel,
God with You

—from Ecclesiastes 4:9–10, 12

Some said they'd pray. Some sent sweet notes. Others called to say they'd heard what happened and wanted me to know their thoughts were with me—which was nice and kind and thoughtful. But you were there. And I couldn't have made it without you.

Some folks brought food or watched the kids or offered a check to help pay the bills—and, of course, I was grateful for each gesture, each love expressed. But, you came through in a different way, at a deeper level.

Like no one else, you were there for me. You let me rant and rave and ramble. Time after time, you sat with me and wiped my tears and washed my cheeks and whispered the words, "I

inspirational message

know. I know. I know." And because of you, I held on.

Sometimes, you let me sit in silence and stare into space, because it seemed the right thing to do. Sometimes you encouraged me to talk. And you'd listen and nod, and your eyes would drip with fresh drops of empathy. You'd let me open up and dump out thoughts I didn't even know I had in me. But, there's one thing you never let me do—give up.

You said I could survive because you are surviving. And for what seems like the thousandth time, you'd hold my hand, look to heaven, and pray for me with the anguish of one who has been there too.

No. I couldn't have made it without you.

Friends are angels who lift our feet when our own wings have trouble remembering how to fly.

—Unknown

If there were such a thing as a pain transfusion, her friend would have willingly volunteered.

There for You

The fog that filled her head refused to clear. Somewhere in the distance, she heard strange, steady beeping and humming sounds—sounds she'd heard before but couldn't quite place. Trying desperately to concentrate, her mind began to drift, *Oh . . . I hurt. I hurt so bad.* She tried to move her arm, but it was too heavy. Now that she thought about it, her whole body felt as if it were encased in cement. She tried to speak, to call out for help, but no sound came.

Hearing voices, she looked up, straining to focus on five sets of eyes looking down at her. One by one, the nurses and doctors hovering above her said, "Hi, Sherry."

She tried to respond, wanting to call out for help, but no sound came. Alarmed by the throbbing pain in her throat, she panicked. *I can't breathe! I can't breathe!* Her breathing

seemed abnormal, and then she realized she wasn't breathing on her own. *Wait! That humming noise is a respirator. Where am I? What's going on?* she silently screamed.

Something terrible had happened. Her memory, though vague, flashed back to sounds of sirens, people asking persistent questions, and the roaring sounds of a helicopter.

Confusion clouded Sherry's mind as she scanned the room for her husband Ken's loving face. *Where is he? What if something is wrong with him? Is he hurt?* Tormenting thoughts engulfed her mind. *Where's my precious Ken?*

Moments later, Ken's dad bent down and whispered words that confirmed her deepest fears, "Kenny's gone."

Sherry inwardly wailed, *No! No! He can't be! Jesus, I need Ken. He can't be gone. How can I live without him?* Soon, the pain medicine took over, and Sherry drifted back to sleep, praying that what she had heard was only a vanishing nightmare.

Later when she awoke, her mother was standing next to her bed, gently holding her IV-pierced hand. "Honey, I'm here for you," her mom assured.

Moments before her mom's arrival, Sherry had despondently thought of dying. But as she looked up at her mother's beautiful smile and loving eyes, Sherry thought, *Jesus, my mother needs me. I can't die now. Please help me.*

Sherry used sign language to spell Ken's name to her mom and struggled to flutter her hand like a bird flying away, symbolizing Ken's death.

"I know, honey. I know," her mom responded sympathetically, patting her hand. Strengthened by her mom's presence, Sherry eventually drifted back to sleep.

Hours later, on the other side of the hospital-room door, Sherry Anne Frattini stood, trying to gather the courage to open the door and walk into the room. She'd come as soon as she'd gotten the news. She and her husband, Mike, had booked airplane tickets from Colorado to Cedar Rapids, Iowa, within hours of the phone call and had hurriedly arranged for someone to care for their children. She could hardly believe that her best friend, Sherry Jones, had been in such a traumatic accident.

The two Sherrys had met sixteen years ago during their junior year at Westminster High School. They were both trying out for the varsity cheerleading squad—Sherry Anne as a returning member of the squad and Sherry as a transfer student. Both girls made the team and instantly connected,

becoming best friends almost overnight. Today, they still lived within thirty miles of each other, frequently interacting on a weekly basis.

And now, her best friend needed her like she had never needed her before.

Sherry and Ken had gone to Iowa for Ken's sister's New Year's Eve wedding. On their way to the airport for the return flight home, Ken's father cautiously slowed the van as he approached an ungated railroad crossing, but a line of dense trees obscured his vision.

By the time they saw the train emerging from behind the trees, it was too late. The train clipped and ripped off the entire right side of the van, sending it into a 360° turn before hurling the vehicle into a ditch.

Ken, his uncle, and Sherry were catapulted more than forty feet from the van into the twenty-below-zero weather. Ken's father and two other relatives suffered only minor cuts and bruises, but Ken and his uncle were pronounced dead at the scene. Unresponsive and barely alive, Sherry was airlifted to a nearby hospital and then quickly rerouted to the University of Iowa Hospital and Clinic, which was better equipped to handle severe trauma injuries.

Sherry's life-threatening injuries included a collapsed

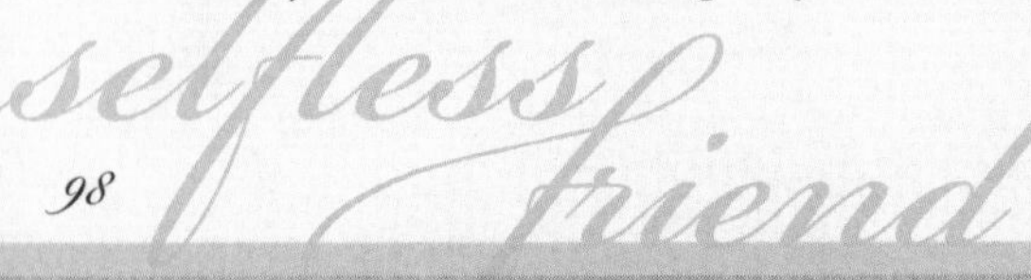

lung, a bruised liver, extensive internal hemorrhaging, and a shattered hip that required eight hours of emergency reconstructive surgery.

Miraculously, she hadn't sustained any spinal cord injury or brain damage, but her body was shattered—she had broken a leg, an arm, three ribs, a clavicle, and her scapula. She also had multiple pelvic fractures and a dislocated shoulder. And to top it all off, Sherry had learned just two months ago that she had cancer.

When Sherry Anne finally stepped into the small, dreary hospital room, her breath caught in her throat when she saw her friend lying motionless on the stiff hospital bed. Surrounded by life-support equipment, oxygen tanks, and flashing monitors, much of Sherry's small frame was entombed in white casts and bandages. Blood oozed through some of the gauze. Metal pins protruded from her right leg, which was raised in traction. What skin was visible was swollen and black and blue. Sherry Anne audibly gasped when she saw the deep, jagged gash across Sherry's knee and leg, exposing the wounded flesh inside.

The octopus of tubes and contraptions extending from her friend's frail body only intensified her fears that she might lose her best friend. What would she do without her

best friend? She needed her! Sherry's eyes were closed, but her intermittent moans revealed that her sleep was not peaceful.

Sherry Anne made her way to her friend's bedside. Tenderly grasping Sherry's hand in hers, she gently squeezed. Sherry opened pain-filled eyes. When she saw her dear friend, her eyes responded with a flicker of recognition. The tube in her throat prevented her from talking, so she feebly motioned for a piece of paper and pen instead. "Ken's dead," she wrote.

"I know, sweetheart. They told me. I'm so sorry. I know how much you loved him." The pain in her best friend's eyes cut through Sherry Anne's heart like a knife. At that moment, Sherry Anne felt she would do anything to make her friend whole again. Thoughts of her own needs fled. "I wish I could take your pain away and put it on me," she said. And she meant it.

And Sherry knew she meant it. If there were such a thing as a pain transfusion, her friend would have willingly volunteered. Knowing that she was loved so completely, so selflessly, sent a surge of courage and hope through Sherry's heart—and for a moment, her fear and depression lifted.

Over the next several days, Sherry Anne took up her

post beside Sherry's mother, who was a constant and faithful support for her daughter. Sherry Anne stayed faithfully by her friend's side, helping her process her thoughts, encouraging her to communicate on paper, and patiently waiting while Sherry painstakingly wrote her needs, feelings, and fears.

And when it came time for Ken's funeral, Sherry Anne stayed by her friend's side. Sherry had waited thirty-one long years to meet and marry Ken. So often she had shared with Sherry Anne that her marriage with Ken far exceeded all her dreams. She had been so content. And now, after only fifteen short months of marriage, he was gone, and Sherry was fighting for her life—denied even the opportunity to find closure with a final good-bye at her husband's funeral. Sherry Anne ached with her friend, feeling the pain of her shattered dreams and unfulfilled future family with Ken. She wished again she could bear some of her beloved friend's pain.

Eventually, it was time for Sherry Anne and her husband to go home. Their children needed them, and she had to get back to college. Although Sherry's condition was improving and the doctors now offered hope, Sherry Anne knew that her friend was not completely out of danger.

Leaving her best friend made her feel as if she were being torn in two.

After returning home, Sherry Anne called every day, getting updates and relaying messages through Sherry's mom.

And then the wonderful day came when Sherry Anne heard the sweet, familiar voice of her friend resonating through the telephone, and she knew in her heart that Sherry was going to make it.

One month after the accident, Sherry stabilized enough to be transferred to a Colorado hospital, only miles from Sherry Anne's home. Again, Sherry Anne was by her side.

One more month, and Sherry was released to go home.

Throughout the healing process, Sherry Anne was there for her friend. She cheered Sherry as she learned to walk on her own. She reminded her how to laugh again. She cried with her when the pain broke through her wall of composure. She helped her grieve and cherish the memories of Ken. She gently rehearsed with her the amazing power of God's grace. And together they celebrated the joy of learning that Sherry's cancer had gone into remission.

Today, Sherry still suffers physical pain from the accident, but she radiates God's faithfulness, sharing with oth-

ers the message that she was "broken, but not forsaken," and she frequently testifies to Solomon's wisdom that "two are better than one."

But as Sherry tells it, a precious moment that lit a flame of hope in her heart was the moment her friend loved her unconditionally and sacrificially and said, "I wish I could take your pain away and put it on me."

seven

faithful friend

My Precious Child,

My all-seeing lamp searches out your very *spirit* and your inmost being. I know the real you that you sometimes try to hide.

I perceive your thoughts and even know what you are going to say before you say it.

If only you realized how *precious* you are to me! I'm continuously thinking good thoughts of you—

thoughts that outnumber all the grains of sand in the entire world.

Thinking fondly of you,

Your Creator

—Proverbs 20:27; Psalm 139

A true friend—

will listen for hours to your side of the story and never once require the facts.

will tell everyone how great you are, even when you've hurt her feelings.

never doubts you love her, even though you haven't called her in eight months.

stocks her pantry with your favorite foods.

knows your middle name but will only use it when she absolutely has to.

will tell you to freshen your lipstick then kindly loan you hers.

will leave crazy messages on your answering machine for no reason at all.

will not embarrass you in public.

will always come when your car breaks down.

always has so much to tell you, even though you've known each other for thirty years.

will go shopping for herself but come home with a gift for you.

inspirational message

carries a good picture of you in her wallet.

will always tell you to follow your heart instead of your head.

remembers wonderful things you did as a child, even though she wasn't there to see them.

would never encourage you to do something stupid.

is the only one who knows where you've hidden the spare key to your house.

will feed your cat while you're gone even if she has allergies.

is the name you always write on your application next to "in case of emergency call_____."

would never talk behind your back even though she'd have plenty to say.

will tell you things you really need to hear, whether you feel like hearing them or not.

comes to you with precious messages like an ambassador from God.

With the death of every friend I love . . . part of me has been buried . . . but their contribution to my being of happiness, strength and understanding remains to sustain me in an altered world.

—Helen Keller

It was one of the hardest things Sunnie had ever done, but it was her way of honoring their friendship.

Last Request

Sunnie and Theresa were like oil and water. If cast for *Gilligan's Island*, Sunnie would play the bubbly Mary Ann—spontaneous and fun yet holding to conservative boundaries—and Theresa would play the gorgeous and flirtatious Ginger—always the center of attention and ready to push life to the limits.

When their brothers introduced them on Halloween night in 1984, Sunnie and Theresa became immediate friends. They even starred together in one of those comical music videos, singing what became their special song—"I Heard It through the Grapevine."

Eventually, Sunnie and Theresa moved into a plush uptown apartment, and these two fast-track, career-geared, materialistic yuppies became intertwined in a friendship that would ultimately alter their destinies.

Donned in their extravagant dresses, there was never a dull moment during their frequent nights on the town. Theresa was a magnet for men, flirtatiously leading them on. Sunnie would try to keep a straight face as Theresa gave alias names and bogus phone numbers. While living a fast, materialistic lifestyle, the hearts of both young women yearned for more.

Sunnie was always mothering Theresa, suggesting she change into a more modest dress or confiscating her keys if she thought her friend had had too much to drink. From the start of their friendship, Theresa teased Sunnie about being a "Holy Roller," but their friendship took a noticeable turn when Sunnie actually became a Christian at a Bible study two years after they met. Her conversion wasn't one of immediate, drastic changes, but it marked the beginning of a gradual makeover of her life and priorities.

While Theresa was respectful of Sunnie's beliefs, she was skeptical of religion as a whole, despite her strong Catholic family upbringing. She wasn't going to invest in something she couldn't see or touch, and she was turned off by hypocritical "Sunday" Christians. She was tolerant, but Christianity definitely wasn't for her. Sunnie was torn: She didn't want to offend Theresa or come across as preachy, yet she longed for her best friend to find the same inner peace she was experiencing. Wanting Theresa to see a difference in her life, Sunnie adopted a low-key witnessing approach. She began doing little things, like setting all the stations in Theresa's car to Christian radio and giving her Christian books to read. But basically, they continued to accept each other "as is."

Neither of them expected Theresa's flirting to lead to a wedding. But in 1988, after Sunnie hoodwinked Theresa into serving as a Junior League Hostess for the delegates at the Republican National Convention in New Orleans, Theresa got the attention of Richard, a campaign operative for one of the presidential candidates.

When Richard accepted their offer to escort them to dinner, Sunnie felt like an intrusive "third wheel." As their threesome continued to spend time together over the next two nights, a slightly competitive rivalry began to develop between the two friends, and Richard became the focal point of their powder-room chats. From the love-sick look in Sunnie's eyes, Theresa accurately assessed that her best friend was falling in love. "Okay. I'll let you have him," Theresa conceded.

The next night, Theresa disappeared so Sunnie and Richard could go out alone. This continued for several

nights, as Richard extended his stay. On the ninth night, he romantically got down on his knee and asked Sunnie to marry him.

The following April, Theresa, forever the faithful friend and good sport, was the maid of honor at Sunnie and Richard's wedding. She couldn't help, however, but teasingly conclude her reception toast with, "And Sunnie, don't ever forget I gave him to you!"

Marriage, distance, and eventually children didn't diminish Sunnie and Theresa's bond. They still talked almost daily, running up three-hundred-dollar phone bills, and frequently flew to visit each other. As Sunnie grew in her faith, her priorities continued to change. Although materialism was losing its grip on Sunnie, it still entangled Theresa.

Two years after their wedding, Richard's rededication to the Lord spurred on Sunnie's faith even more, and she became more bold in telling Theresa how God was changing her. In May of 1996, they met for dinner at a midway point between their distant homes. Shaken by the recent death of a friend, Theresa was in a somber, reflective mood. After a heavy discussion of death, Sunnie candidly blurted out, "Hey frogface, you have to promise that if I die you'll marry Richard and take care of my three kids."

Laughing at Sunnie's bizarre request, Theresa countered with a request of her own. "Well, my worst nightmare is that I'll look ugly in my coffin. I'd just die if they put me in some icky pale dress and my hair was a frazzled mess. You have to promise me that I'll go out in style!"

Getting serious again, Sunnie handed Theresa a book explaining what different churches believe. As they teasingly pushed the book back and forth between each other, Sunnie said, "Girlfriend, read this and pick a church." She was absolutely dumbfounded when Theresa nonchalantly responded, "Hey, how come in all of these years, you've never given me a Bible?"

After dinner, Sunnie immediately embarked on a search for a Bible bookstore. Together they picked out matching Bibles and Stephen Curtis Chapman tapes.

It was a night Sunnie would never forget. Sitting in Theresa's flashy black 1996 convertible Corvette parked in the driveway of Sunnie's sister's house, it finally happened: After years of praying for and witnessing to Theresa, Sunnie had the privilege of leading her best friend to the Lord.

They talked past midnight in the intimate, spiritual dimension Sunnie had always prayed for. "Come on, spend the night," Sunnie urged her friend. Theresa declined, saying she needed to go home, so they exchanged big hugs and tearful good-byes. They both understood that their close friendship had moved to a deeper level.

On Mother's Day, just two weeks later, Sunnie was out when Theresa's boyfriend called. When Sunnie came home, Richard greeted her at the door with the tragic news: Theresa had been killed in a car accident.

For a few moments, she disregarded the call as a cruel hoax. But as the tears started rolling down Richard's face, she realized that she had truly lost her soul mate. "Theresa was just starting her new life! How can this be?" she tearfully asked. Consoling each other in embrace, they cried, remembering the dear friend who had brought their lives together.

Later, Sunnie drove to Theresa's hometown and met Theresa's sister, Verlin, to help make the funeral arrangements. When Sunnie viewed the matronly light peach dress with a high lacy collar that had been delivered for Theresa's burial, she braced herself to execute her friend's unusual last request. "Please don't take offense, but Theresa would kill me if she were buried in this." With Verlin's blessings, Sunnie got to work.

She spent over two hours restoring her best friend's curls, as Theresa's recent perm had been reduced to strawlike conditions by the embalming chemicals. She spruced up Theresa's lips with bright red lipstick and dressed her in her own favorite red-tailored suit, which Theresa had often borrowed, along with her pearl earrings and necklace. It was one of the hardest things Sunnie had ever done, but it was her way of honoring their friendship. When she completed the makeover, she almost sensed Theresa laughing from heaven. She even arranged to have their special "I Heard It through the Grapevine" video played at the wake.

During the eulogy, Sunnie had the opportunity to stand up and share about the life-changing decision that Theresa had made during her final weeks. Afterward, almost two dozen people approached Sunnie to thank her for sharing and to say that they wanted that kind of new life too.

At the graveside farewell, Sunnie experienced a roller coaster of emotions. While she rejoiced that Theresa was with Jesus, it was inconceivably hard to say good-bye to the person who knew everything about her yet still loved and accepted her. Daring to be vulnerable, they had shared

things they had never told anyone else—and now those secrets were being buried with her trusted friend. But the blessings of their unmasked friendship and special memories, especially their last tender moments together, would be a sweet source of comfort to her lonely, lump-filled heart until their heavenly reunion.

hugs™ for friends book 2

Stories, Sayings, and Scriptures to Encourage and Inspire

G. A. Myers
Personalized scriptures by
LeAnn Weiss

CONTENTS

Chapter One: Timing 127

Chapter Two: Companionship 145

Chapter Three: Commitment 163

Chapter Four: Involvement 181

Chapter Five: Sacrifice. 197

Chapter Six: Dependability 215

Chapter Seven: Faithfulness 231

In the sweetness
of friendship let there be
laughter, and sharing
of pleasures. For in the dew
of little things the heart finds
its morning and is refreshed.

Kahlil Gibran

Chapter One

Timing

the selecting of the best time
or speed for doing something in order to
achieve the desired or maximum result

*L*ift your eyes up
and *remember* that your
help comes from *Me*.

I take hold
of your right *hand*
and remind you not to fear
because *I will help* you.

*W*atch Me make all things
beautiful
in My perfect timing.

Almighty God

LOVING YOU,

Your Almighty God

—from Psalm 121:1–2; Isaiah 41:13; Ecclesiastes 3:11

The Scriptures say that God saved us "*at just the right time*" (Romans 5:6). He knows the importance of timing. That's why He sends us the friends we need at just the right time—to fill the gaps, hear our gripes, and strengthen us when we want to give up.

Is there anything more pleasant than the voice of a friend when we're feeling the full weight of failure and frustration? That sound alone can bring hope to a surrendered heart.

Is there anything more comforting than the arm of a friend steadying us when we become weak-kneed from the stress and strain of life's weight on our shoulders? That helpful arm serves to remind us that we don't have to face tomorrow alone.

inspirational message

Friends seem to appear out of nowhere when we need them most—to reinforce us for unexpected or extended battle. They come without fear for themselves, because they know sacrifice is part of the friendship. They come to walk with us, side by side and step by step, until we find a way to defeat the enemy.

Every time a friend rescues us at just the right time, another memory is made. Celebrate those memories often. Lift those diamond-bright moments to the light and be thankful for the pressures that brought them into existence. Above all, don't forget to thank God. He was the one who knew exactly the right time to send you a friend.

*G*od pairs people as friends

at the right time and

pace and season of need.

Wayne Watson

Though Kim was taken aback by Sherry's brashness and honesty, she found herself drawn to her.

A Friend in the Clutch

It started on a chilly, windy day in Wichita, Kansas. The two young women didn't plan to get to know each other well, much less become good friends. Kim Logan was rushing from her apartment to her car to get to class at Wichita State University. She had the biggest exam of the semester in fifteen minutes, and she wanted to get there in time to look over her notes again. Distracted with juggling her books while reviewing in her mind what she had stayed up half the night to study, she didn't notice Sherry Brown until she bumped into her. Sherry was rubbing sleep from her heavy-lidded brown eyes and stretching in preparation for the mile walk to her first class of the day.

The girls were acquainted. Sherry lived downstairs in the red brick apartment complex, and Kim lived on the upper level right above her. Until today, their only real interaction had been several small confrontations over Sherry's music, which was always too loud for Kim. That was the number one reason Kim didn't plan to get to know Sherry better. Sherry liked her music the way she liked her life: loud, fun, and full of flare. Her major was marketing, and she liked the fast pace that accompanied her creative opportunities.

Kim, on the other hand, was a self-proclaimed nerd majoring in English literature. She loved solitude, meditation, prayer, and reading. Her idea of a great weekend was walking through quiet woods and talking to God or curling up with a hefty classic tome, which, she suspected, Sherry would find useful only as a doorstop.

On her way to the car that day, Kim made a halfhearted stab at being friendly and said hello to Sherry. Never shy,

Sherry took the opportunity to ask for a ride to the campus. Caught off guard, Kim hesitated for just a moment, then agreed. "OK," she said, then added quickly, "but I control the volume on the radio."

"As long as we don't have to listen to Bach or BEEthoven," Sherry laughed, exaggerating for fun.

"I'm surprised you even know they existed," Kim shot back.

"Oooooh," Sherry responded. "That was witty, Miss Kim. There may be hope for you—you could have a sense of humor behind those wire-rimmed glasses!"

"For someone begging a ride, you're pretty lippy," Kim remarked.

"You're right, there," Sherry admitted honestly. "In fact, 'Lippy' is my middle name. My mom tells me that if she had a nickel for every time I mouthed off, she'd be a millionaire. I'm sorry. If I promise to tone it down a bit, could I still have that ride?"

Though Kim was taken aback first by Sherry's brashness and then by her honesty, she found herself drawn to Sherry.

"Sure, but I still get to control the radio." The two shared a chuckle.

Kim slid into the driver's seat of the Toyota Celica and turned the key. The engine didn't roar to life as she expected it to. It was so silent she could hear the click of the key turning in the ignition. "What in the world…" Kim trailed off, puzzled.

Sherry covered her face with her hands. "Uh-oh," she said softly. "Check your lights. You probably left them on all night."

Amazed at Sherry's instinctive response, Kim glanced at the knob and realized Sherry was right. "Oh no," Kim moaned. "What'll I do? I can't miss that test!"

Tears formed in Kim's eyes as she hastily grabbed her books. She'd have to run the mile to campus.

"Hey, hold on there, Kimmy," Sherry said as if she were pulling back the reins of a horse. "Don't you know you can start a stick shift by popping the clutch?"

Kim looked at her with a puzzled expression. "No, I've never even heard of popping a clutch."

"What was I thinking! Guys like Twain and Dickens don't write about things like that," Sherry said with good-natured sarcasm. "Here's how it's done: I'll get out and push the car until it picks up a little speed while you sit there and hold the clutch in. When I yell 'pop the clutch,' you let it out fast, and it'll start right up. Got it?"

"I think so," Kim replied with genuine awe.

Sherry got behind the car and went through a checklist with Kim. "First gear, check?"

Kim shouted back, "Check!"

"Brake off, check?" Sherry continued.

"Check!" Kim echoed loudly.

"Clutch in, check?" Sherry finished.

"Check!" Kim shouted.

"All systems are go!" Sherry yelled cheerfully.

Sherry pushed with all of her might, and the car began to creep forward, slowly at first, then picking up speed. Kim sat frozen in her seat until Sherry screamed at the top of her lungs, "Pop the stupid clutch!"

As soon as Kim complied, the car lurched forward and

startled her so badly she slammed on the brakes. Sherry went flying up onto the trunk of the car. A frightened Kim looked in her rearview mirror to see Sherry, red-faced, sprawled across the trunk and on the rear window.

"Are you all right?" Kim yelled. "I'm so sorry, Sherry. I'm so sorry!"

To her shock and relief, Kim discovered that Sherry was laughing hysterically. "That was absolutely the shabbiest attempt at clutch-popping I've ever witnessed," Sherry gasped between outbursts of laughter.

Emerging from the car, Kim joined in the laughter. "It was pretty comical to see you take flight and land on my trunk that way," she told Sherry, making an arc through the air with one hand.

"Yeah, I'm sure I looked like a bird."

"More like an airborne ostrich. Your legs were everywhere!"

They laughed for several minutes before Sherry spoke with mock indignation. "Hey, why am I laughing?" she harrumphed. "I just realized you let the car die. Now we have to do the whole thing over again."

They looked at each other for a split second, then screamed with laughter again.

Kim looked sheepishly at Sherry. "Do you want me to push this time and let you pop the clutch?"

"No, Kimmy, my friend," Sherry said patiently. "I want you to learn to get it right. Hop back in there, and let's try it again."

They went through the checklist one more time with an added reminder to keep the car running after Kim popped the clutch. Then Sherry started pushing. "Pop the clutch, girl, pop the clutch," she yelled.

This time Kim performed her task perfectly, and the engine roared to life.

Sherry hopped into the car and rubbed her palms together gleefully. "You'll never learn that in one of your books," she told Kim, who nodded in agreement.

"You know," Sherry continued thoughtfully, "I can tell you need taking care of. I think I'll nominate myself for the job. You live in a world of books and imagination where smart people express ideas in words. I live in the real world where people have to be street-smart. I could use some help with my study skills, and trust me, you could use some tips on your social skills," she giggled, teasingly. "Let's get you to class. After all, you can't miss the most important test of the year."

After class they met for lunch—an appointment that soon turned into a daily event. Their respect for each other grew as each helped the other discover a world she never knew existed. They dreamed together, hoped together, and always took care of each other. Together they built a friendship that would last a lifetime.

Whenever differences threatened their closeness, they would recall the morning when two opposite personalities became lifelong friends over a stalled car and a popped clutch, and they would laugh until they cried.

Chapter Two

Companionship

the state of being with someone;
the relationship as companions

When you come near to Me,
I'm so *close* to you.

There's no darkness in Me.
I fill you with *joy*
in My presence and *bless you*
with *eternal* pleasures
at My right hand.

May you walk in
My *light*,
experiencing *sweet* fellowship
with friends
as My Son's blood
purifies you.

Father of Light

Shining on you,

Your Father of Light

—from James 4:8; Psalm 16:11; 1 John 1:5–7

No modern medicine or meditation has quite the same healing effect as a friend. Friends can take the space once occupied by loneliness and fill it to the brim with partnership and purpose. Isolation is replaced by delightful companionship. Heartache is healed by the joy and satisfaction of camaraderie.

Only a soul mate can fill the need in each of us for true companionship—the craving to be known, understood, and valued. And that kind of friendship is a rare gift. But when that treasure is found, it works its way into our lives, into the deepest recesses of our hearts. Companionship can transform us. It replaces selfishness with a spirit of sacrifice. It soothes the sadness of loss and raises a song of joy. It buries the hatchet of hatred and reaps a harvest of love.

inspirational message

The wonderful, miraculous thing about friendship is, anyone can participate. Each of us has the power to partner with another and, in so doing, change the world one heart at a time. You, as a friend, have that power. Your companionship can bring peace and joy to another.

Companionship does require an investment. It takes time to build. You'll have to share your pain and loss, even reveal your weaknesses. But the rewards are worth it, because companionship means not only bearing one another's burdens but also sharing in victories, in healing, in joy. And in a world fueled by greed, selfishness, and hatred, friendship—companionship—may be the only way to make a difference.

A friend is someone

who shares with you a smile,

a tear, a hand.

Conover

*T*he thought of living without her friend brought waves of anxiety and desperation.

Toe to Toe

Helen stood and gazed longingly out the glassed wall that stretched all the way up to the cathedral ceiling in her great room. It was Thanksgiving and darkness had already begun to cling to the freshly fallen snow. She could see the different hues of light thrown off by neighboring houses that were already covered with the small multicolor lights that blinked and danced in the night and signaled the coming of Christmas. Although this was normally one of her favorite times of year, she could find no reason for joy now. She felt alone, unwanted, and dispirited. Her best friend had died six weeks earlier, and she was having a hard time adjusting to the silence and the sadness. She tugged absently at her shoulder-length gray hair and thought about Connie.

Connie was more than a friend; she was a soul mate and confidante who had faced the best and worst of times with Helen. They had met at St. Andrews Hospital fifteen years earlier when Helen's husband, Harley, was being treated for cancer. Connie was a volunteer who loved bringing some measure of comfort to the patients and their families. She had taken up the job after her own husband died of cancer, and she was deeply loved and appreciated in the hospital by staff and patients alike.

Helen, however, didn't much like Connie when they first met. The tall Texan was loud and loving, but Helen was a quiet southern belle not given to boisterous displays of affection. She shunned Connie's attempts at friendship by ignoring her. That, however, only fueled Connie's determination. Connie brought small gifts and hugged her even though Helen wouldn't respond. Connie would tap her toe three times on the top of Helen's toe and say, "When you get tired of carrying your heartache alone, we can walk through it together." Helen would simply lower her eyes until Connie walked away.

Yet when Harley's struggle with cancer ended, Helen felt so alone and overwhelmed that she turned to Connie for comfort. "I can't bear this alone. Would you help me get through it?" she pleaded softly. Without saying a word, Connie tapped the familiar three times on her toe, then gathered Helen in a gentle hug. This time, Helen crumpled into Connie's arms and wept for an hour.

After that the two became close friends and partners in encouragement. Anytime a need arose in the small town, the two of them pitched in to help. Helen and Connie came to respect and treasure their different personalities. They enjoyed volunteering together so much that after about a year, they decided to sell their respective homes and purchase one together so they could be closer to the hospital and could open their home to parents of children who were undergoing treatment. Time with Connie was full of friendship, fun, and fruitful labor. The two women were like children, laughing loudly, playing good-natured pranks, and doing good deeds.

At Christmastime last year, Connie began showing the first signs of her illness. It didn't stop them from delivering the gifts they had gathered for needy children in the area, but by New Year's Day, Connie was feeling weak. The next Monday she consulted her doctor, who sent her to the hospital for testing. The diagnosis was devastating. Connie had advanced colon cancer.

Connie faced her future with courage, but Helen struggled. At times the thought of living life without her friend brought waves of anxiety and desperation. Connie almost always sensed her panic and would tap her slippered foot softly on Helen's toe. "We'll walk through this together, my friend," she promised.

It was early October when Connie neared the end of her battle. Helen made her as comfortable as possible, but Connie's concern was that Helen not be lonely or lose what had become her purpose in life. One afternoon she asked Helen to bring her the phone and leave her alone. About two hours later, she called her friend back into the room.

"What were you doing in here all that time?" Helen quizzed her.

Connie slid her leg from the bed, tapped her toe on Helen's, and said, "Don't worry, my friend. We'll walk through this together."

One week later, Connie died peacefully in her sleep. Helen tried to keep up the good work she and Connie had done together, but each day her grief and loneliness made it harder and harder until she finally retreated into the quiet shelter of her home.

Now, on Thanksgiving, she felt the full weight of her grief. The loneliness left her feeling more desolate than ever. Suddenly a sharp knock on the front door echoed through the empty house. At first she tried to ignore it. The knock came again, louder. Helen looked out her front window to see a young man in a snowy beard, overalls, and heavy boots standing at her door with two large packages.

She opened the door slightly and saw on the street a white van with the words "Heavenly Ham" painted on the side. "Mrs. Chamberlain?" The man asked hesitantly. "Helen Chamberlain?"

"Yes, I'm Helen Chamberlain," she answered with reservation.

"I'm sure glad your home, ma'am. I've got three turkeys and fixings enough for an army out here in the van." He stepped into the house with two wrapped turkeys before she could object.

"There must be some mistake—I didn't order any turkeys, and I certainly don't need three of them," Helen protested.

"No, I know you didn't order them. Connie Howser ordered them almost two months ago and said they were to be delivered at 5 P.M. sharp on Thanksgiving Day."

Helen looked as though she had just seen an angel. "Connie called you and did what?"

"Yes ma'am, she gave strict instructions about everything. She said they were to be here right at five o'clock because a bunch of people would be here for Thanksgiving dinner." Placing the turkeys on the table, the man looked around with a puzzled expression. "Did people forget to come, ma'am?"

"No, I didn't invite anyone," Helen answered sharply.

Embarrassed, the deliveryman excused himself to get the rest of the meal from the truck.

"Just what are you up to, Connie Howser?" Helen whispered to herself.

The young man returned with arms laden. "I think your guests have arrived," he announced.

Helen rushed to the door and opened it to see Amy, a nurse from the cancer ward, leading a crowd of people up the sidewalk to the house. When she reached the door she smiled broadly and said, "Hey, Helen, Connie invited all the families in the cancer ward, along with any patients who felt up to it, to come over for Thanksgiving dinner. She said you'd have it all set up and I would disappoint you terribly if I didn't bring everyone I could."

Amy noticed tears spilling down Helen's face and whispered, "You OK, Helen?"

"Oh yes, I'm fine. Come on in here and get warm. The food is being set up now, and we can give thanks and eat in just a few minutes."

Helen stepped away into another room and spoke as though Connie were there with her. "Thank you for the gift, my friend. I feel the tap of your toe."

She looked back at the crowd that had gathered in the living room where she and Connie had comforted so many grieving friends and families. Dozens of guests stood or sat, some with blank stares, others wringing their hands, still others with worry etched in their faces. Helen wiped away her tears and entered the room with a hearty smile.

"Welcome, my friends. I'm glad to have you here on this Thanksgiving Day, and I want all of you to feel free to visit again whenever you need a friend to help carry your load. My name is Helen, and I'll be that friend."

After a prayer of thanks the group began moving into the dining room. One woman stayed behind, staring out the window. She was middle-aged and thin, with shoulders that sagged under the weight of her sorrow. Helen quietly joined her and asked her name.

"Darla Hayes," the woman answered softly, reluctantly. "My husband is in the hospital and probably won't make it through Christmas. I don't even know what I'm doing here."

Helen remembered the pain she had felt when she lost her husband, and she remembered how Connie had helped her make it through. She took Darla gently by the shoulders and turned her so she could look into her eyes. "You may not know why you're here, but I do." She tapped her toe on Darla's and said, "Don't worry. We'll walk through this together."

Chapter Three

Commitment

a pledge or promise;
obligation

Experience My everlasting arms.
My *Spirit* made you,
and My **breath** gives you *life*.

I am your **trustworthy** refuge.
When you make *Me*
and **My** ways your **priority**,
I'll take care of all your needs
through My unlimited **riches** in *glory*.

And don't forget…
you can do *all things*
because *Christ* is your unfailing
power
source.

Heavenly Father

HOLDING YOU,

Your Heavenly Father

—from Deuteronomy 33:27; Job 33:4; Philippians 4:13, 19

What is it that makes you the best of friends? What is it about you that brings out the best in others?

It could be your willingness to engage the lives of your friends wherever they are. You willingly enter their war zones and fight the daily battles with words of encouragement and comfort. No fight is too small or too big for you when it comes to your friends.

It could be the help you offer others climbing the mountain of faith. You anchor those pushing themselves to the summit. You refuse to leave anyone behind. You won't give up until everyone reaches the goal.

Perhaps most important is the deep connection you eagerly seek to have with others. It's an invisible link of friendship that unites your heart with the hearts of others. It's powerful enough to hold lives together no matter what may come along. Nothing can shake you loose from those you call friends. No one can come between you and those you love. Nothing can separate you.

In a world of shallow commitments and abandoned loyalties, your devotion is unique and rare. You are locked in for the long haul. You're staying no matter who else goes. You've wrapped yourself around the hearts of your friends with an embrace that will hold through any storm.

What is it that makes you the best of friends? The answer is simple: commitment. Your commitment to others makes you a friend par excellence!

Real friendship is shown in times of trouble.

Euripides

Sam rammed his car into the speeding auto, pushing it into the median before it could reach the children.

Blood Brothers

Three weathered men shuffled into the downtown doughnut shop with tired faces and swollen eyes. They had many good reasons for congregating every Tuesday morning for their favorite brew and pastry, but the thing that summoned these long-term friends today was not good and not welcome. Someone was missing. Someone with whom they had served in World War II on a bomber they had christened the *Wind Walker.*

The first man, Alton, had been a gunner, and a mighty good one, to hear the old men talk. He could wedge his thin frame into the tightest crevice and still find room to maneuver. He hadn't changed much through the years. He had gained just ten pounds since his air force days, and his youthful spirit still shone from his ocean-blue eyes.

Sonny, the other gunner, had not fared as well. Although he had retained his athletic physique, he bore the marks of a hard life—lines of care were etched deeply in his face.

Blake was the youngest, and he looked it. The navigator for the flying fortress possessed unusual energy and an infectious laugh.

Each ordered their "usual" and found a seat. "I want to order one for Sam," Sonny announced. "It's just not the same without him. Maybe it'll make him feel closer." Sonny went to the counter and requested one more coffee and doughnut, just the way Sam would have ordered it.

Sam's absence was the reason for their shared sorrow. He had been the pilot of the great bomber they'd flown for two years. He had remained the leader of this band of veterans ever since. It was he who initiated the routine of visiting the neighborhood coffee shop to relive the old stories. But today he couldn't join them. Sam was in the hospital, fighting for his life.

It had been more an act of heroism than an accident. Sam had been driving on the busy interstate. A drunk driver was weaving dangerously. Sam looked ahead and saw a school bus stalled by the side of the road and surrounded by children. The erratic car was careening directly toward the kids.

With the keen skills and instincts of a pilot, Sam rammed his car into the side of the speeding auto, pushing it into the median before it could reach the children. With a thundering crash, Sam's car flipped over, then came to rest right-side up.

The teacher who witnessed the incident told emergency workers that Sam had saved their lives. No one could yet tell whether the unconscious hero had done so at the cost of his own life. When Sam's wife, Lil, called Alton with the news, he'd called the friends together. They had kept vigil at the hospital while they waited for news from Sam's surgeon.

They knew Sam would have despised their "creative conversation" while time passed in the waiting room. Sam had saved each of their lives in separate incidents during the war. Every time they shared their favorite stories, Sam noticed that his comrades got more "creative" in how they remembered the details. He once told them that if he were half the man they made him out to be, he wouldn't have needed a plane—he could have just flapped his arms, dropped bombs from his armpits, and won the war single-handedly.

But Alton, Sonny, and Blake knew that Sam really had saved their necks on many occasions, and no amount of humility on his part would make them forget it or stop recounting it. The three of them had been afraid that they'd never get a chance to return Sam's favors. Now they all felt powerless to help the friend who lay near death.

It was nearly midnight when the surgeon came to talk with the anxious group about Sam's prognosis. The news was bleak. Sam was bleeding internally, and they were having difficulty pinpointing the problem. Sam needed a transfusion fast.

At this news, everyone in the room took a deep breath. Lil and the friends knew what it meant. Sam had an extremely rare blood type. The small-town hospital had none on hand.

They had already begun searching for possible donors in the area. Within thirty minutes the answer came, but with little comfort. One donor, Lloyd Simpson, lived an hour north in the tiny community of Portland, but every attempt to reach him had been fruitless.

Blake spoke up first. "Let's get in a car and go after this guy," he urged the others. "We owe it to Sam to find him and get him here."

"It'll be two o'clock in the morning by the time we get there," Sonny protested. "What are we going to do, roust this guy out of bed and drag him to the hospital?"

Alton and Blake looked at each other. In unison, they said, "That's exactly what we'll do."

Chapter Three: *commitment*

The three friends piled into Alton's Buick Roadmaster. They peeled out of the parking lot and headed for Portland on their most important mission in nearly sixty years. They would do whatever it took to bring Sam home safely.

It was 0200 when the three hit the sleepy town of Portland. The three shadowy figures who emerged from the car didn't hesitate. They were like children having decided to jump into a freezing mountain spring. They headed for the house, their faces firmly set toward the door.

Alton rang the doorbell and knocked until a light appeared within. A gruff voice challenged them through the door. "What in the world do you want? Do you realize what time it is?"

Blake was undeterred. "Is your name Lloyd Simpson?"

"Yes, what of it?"

"We have a friend who needs your blood," Sonny spoke plainly.

"Mr. Simpson," Blake tried to explain. "We have a friend who served with us in World War II. He saved our lives. Now he's lying in the hospital near death because they don't have the blood to match his rare type. His blood's the same as yours, Mr. Simpson," Blake continued, his voice choked with emotion. "You're the only one who can help him. If you don't come with us, Sam Shepherd won't live through the night."

Suddenly the door flew open and Lloyd Simpson emerged. "Would that be the same Sam Shepherd who piloted the *Wind Walker*?" he asked.

Three surprised friends shouted in unison, "Yes!"

Lloyd disappeared again, leaving the men standing dumbfounded on the steps. In a minute he reappeared wearing a robe, moving at full speed, and bellowing, "What are we waiting for? Let's get going. We have a hero to save."

On the way to the hospital, Lloyd showed them a picture of himself with Sam standing in front of the *Wind Walker*'s hangar. Lloyd had been a mechanic at the air base. He had never forgotten Sam because once, when he had been seriously wounded, Sam had come to his rescue. It was Sam's blood that had sustained Lloyd's life. He could scarcely believe that now, after all these years, he would have the chance to return the favor.

Chapter Three: *commitment*

It was nearly four o'clock in the morning when the Roadmaster reached the hospital with its precious cargo. Sam was fading fast when the doctors rushed Lloyd in for the transfusion.

Several more hours passed before the doctor appeared with a cautious smile on her weary face, bearing the news that Sam's bleeding had finally stopped. But he wasn't out of the woods yet.

Now it was early in the morning—just a few hours after their middle-of-the-night mission to save Sam's life—when they gathered to wait for news at their favorite coffee shop. They had just raised their cups when Alton's cell phone rang. Answering it with a timid hello, his face soon broke into a big smile. "He's all right then?" Alton laughed in relief.

He hung up the phone, then dialed the number for Lloyd, who had since been released from the hospital. "Lloyd?" he said after a moment of silence. "I wanted you to get the news when we all did. Sam is going to be fine." They all erupted in cheers.

When they settled down, Alton continued: "Sam's wife told him what you did for him, Lloyd. He wants us to stop by during visiting hours. He wants you to come too. He also told me to ask you one more thing: What are you doing on Tuesday mornings?"

Chapter Four

Involvement

a sense of concern with
and curiosity about
someone or something

You don't have to *fear* evil.
I *restore* your soul and
prepare **blessings** for you
in the *presence* of your enemies.

Because I **help** you,
you won't be disgraced.
I am your **sun** and your **shield**,
giving you *grace* and *glory*.

In the **shelter** of My presence,
I hide you
from the **intrigues** of people
and *protect* you
from false accusations.

God of Truth

DEFENDING YOU,

Your God of Truth

PS Remember, I am for you! Who can be against you?

—from Psalm 23:3–5; Isaiah 50:7;
Psalms 84:11; 31:20; Romans 8:31

Do you know what your friends say about you? You may be surprised. They may not talk much about your looks or your charm. They probably don't even focus on your taste in clothes or the car you drive. No, when your friends talk about you, they speak about different qualities. Perhaps they describe you as having eyes that are always watchful; you never miss a thing when it comes to friends who are in need. Your eyes are constantly on the lookout for ways to serve and protect those for whom you care.

Or maybe they comment on your hands—how busy they are, always waving to neighbors, greeting new people and inviting them into your world. Your hands never seem still; they are actively engaged in offering needed affection or comfort.

They might even describe your feet as being swift, running toward tragedy or heartbreak, getting you there first and without fail. And when you arrive, your bright and sympathetic smile warms the heart and welcomes the hurting.

What may surprise you the most is how many of your friends notice your voice: calming when the storms of doubt arise; encouraging when others are weary; inspiring when someone's courage begins to falter; hopeful when goals and dreams seem hard to attain.

Oh, sure, you're nice looking, smart, maybe even witty—but your friends recognize that your most valuable quality is your willingness to get involved in the lives of others. To make a difference. To be a friend.

A true friend provides a safe haven. She accepts us, failures, foibles, and all. She does not judge us when we show her who we are. She responds with gentleness and empathy. She is genuinely on our team.

Ann Hibbard

Elizabeth ran down the steps and into the street, arriving just as the young driver pulled a baseball bat from his backseat and started for the older man.

Friendly Intervention

To look at Elizabeth, you'd think she was sugar sweet and calm spirited. Everyone who knew her well would agree…to a point. Elizabeth Kilcher, with black hair reaching down to her shoulder blades, large brown eyes, delicate frame, and quick step, was genuinely kind and easygoing. But on a warm July evening, two strangers were about to find out what Elizabeth's friends and family already knew.

It was just about dusk in the small suburb of St. Louis, Missouri. Elizabeth was washing the dinner dishes and gazing out her kitchen window overlooking the street in front of her house. She loved to look at the beautiful yard sculpted and nurtured by her husband, Stan. That evening, he had gone to an important meeting with the leadership of their church. Elizabeth stayed behind with their two sons, who were watching their favorite program on television in the living room.

Suddenly Elizabeth heard the ugly sound of metal crunching and folding, like the sound of one of her boys flattening an empty soda can. She caught a glimpse of two cars at the intersection just down the street. As she leaned in closer to the window, she saw two men step out of their cars. One looked to be in his late forties, dressed in khaki slacks and a denim shirt. He towered over the other, younger man who glared back at him. The boy couldn't have been more than eighteen years old. He wore baggy blue jeans, a black-and-white T-shirt with "No Fear" printed on it, and a scowl that spelled trouble.

Elizabeth could tell that the two were yelling at each other about the fact that the older man had rear-ended the young man's car. It was clearly the older man's fault, since the teenager was stopped at the intersection waiting for his turn to proceed. Their argument was escalating to fever pitch, and if allowed to continue, it looked as though it would end in violence.

Elizabeth dashed into the living room and instructed the boys to stay put; she had to go outside and would be right back. But her agitated tone made the boys lose all interest in the program and follow her outside to see what was going on. From their front porch, the family heard a fountain of profanity from the older man. He was denying responsibility for the accident and blaming the young man for not pulling out sooner.

The young driver's verbal counterattack had a harshness and intensity that made Elizabeth's hair stand on end. The older man said something derogatory about the boy's mother. The young man's face flushed a terrible shade of red, and he turned back and walked swiftly toward his car.

In a flash Elizabeth sensed what he was doing. Until then, she'd been unsure whether she should get involved in this scene. Now she knew she had to step in. She ran down the steps, across the small front yard, and into the street, arriving at the scene just as the young driver pulled a baseball bat from his backseat and started for the older man. Elizabeth stepped in between them, placed both hands against the boy's chest, and leaned hard to keep him from advancing farther. "Son, I don't know you, but I'm telling you right now that you don't want to ruin your life by assaulting the likes of this guy."

The teenager, with angry tears forming in his eyes and pronounced veins throbbing in his neck, spoke through clenched teeth. "He said something about my mother that I can't let him say."

"I know," Elizabeth said, trying to calm him. "I heard him myself. But his behavior doesn't give you the right to physically attack him. Look at him," she said, nodding red-faced toward the other driver. "He's old enough to know better, and yet he talks and acts like some irresponsible child."

"Hey, lady, what business is this of yours?" the man piped up, insulted.

Elizabeth swung around to face the man, pointed up to her porch and said, "You see those boys up there? Well, I'm their mother, and I will not have you invading their world with anger and language they shouldn't have to hear."

The man scowled with anger at his injured pride and aimed a challenge at the boy: "Come on with that bat, if you want to!" The boy surged forward, but Elizabeth was once more able to block him and hold him off.

"Listen," she spoke more firmly this time. "Your mother, whom you're defending, would tell you to back off—not to attack this idiot, because he's not worth it. You don't want to throw away your future on him, do you?" she pleaded, now holding his gaze and speaking more gently.

The young man looked into Elizabeth's sincere brown eyes and saw his own mother's care reflected in them. Realizing she was right, he turned sullenly and headed back to his car.

Elizabeth turned once more toward the older man and scolded him: "You ought to be ashamed of yourself, assaulting this boy with such profanity. She waved her hand around, indicating the neighbors who had gathered. Everyone can see that the accident was your fault.

"Grace, call the police," she shouted to her elderly friend across the street. Elizabeth wasn't about to leave until the situation was completely diffused. She then left the man by his car and walked back to talk with the teenager once more.

By now the young driver's anger had subsided, and other emotions took its place. "Thank you, ma'am," he repeated over and over as tears streamed down his face. "If you hadn't been here, I know I would have killed him. I just know I would have killed him."

Elizabeth learned that the young man's name was Kevin, that his mother had recently died after a long illness, and that Kevin had been struggling to adjust after the loss. She tried to comfort him. "Kevin, your mom would have been proud of the choice you made today."

After the police ticketed the older man and both drivers left the scene, Elizabeth walked back to her home to the applause of everyone who had witnessed her courage. This was the Elizabeth they had come to know—someone who would intervene in any situation where someone was in need—especially in need of a friend and advocate.

Elizabeth didn't consider her work done, however. She started shopping at the grocery store where Kevin worked so she could check on him and offer support and encouragement. Kevin always made sure he was the one to carry out Elizabeth's groceries so he could have a chance to update her on what was going on in his life. The two became good friends, always sharing a short prayer together before they parted. Many times Kevin would close her car door and lean down to the window, not wanting anyone else to see his misty eyes, and say, "Thanks again, Mrs. Kilcher, for being there when I needed you the most."

"Friends look out for each other," she would always answer, smiling warmly. "That's just what we do."

Chapter Five

Sacrifice

forfeiture of something highly valued
for the sake of one considered
to have a greater value or claim

Because of My incomparable
love for you,
I made the ultimate sacrifice,
giving up My *Son*.

You can trust
Me to *graciously* give
you all things.

Love each other
as *I've loved* you.
Love others sincerely and *deeply*,
honoring others above yourself.
Real love is patient and kind
and isn't *self-seeking*.

The hidden blessing is that
when you *delight* yourself in Me,
I give you the very things
your heart truly *desires*.

King and Friend

GIVING MYSELF FOR YOU,

Your King and Friend

—from Romans 8:32; 1 John 4:7; 1 Peter 1:22;
Romans 12:10; 1 Corinthians 13:4–5; Psalm 37:4

Self-sacrifice is the defining pinnacle of friendship. Jesus said, "*Greater love has no one than this, that he lay down his life for his friends*" (John 15:13).

We're not often called upon to sacrifice our lives for our friends, but the principle of sacrifice remains true today. If you have friends you know would brave a burning car to pull you to safety or face down an angry mob that was after your blood, you can count yourself blessed indeed. But sacrifice is so much more than being willing to die for a friend.

It's being willing to die *with* your friend when the crowd condemns or ridicules your ideas. It's accommodating your craving for Chinese when she's secretly dying for pizza. It's driving across town three times a day to let your dog out so you can have a romantic weekend away. It's giving you the best seat at the movies, the bigger piece of French silk pie, and taking vacation to accompany you to the doctor for that scary test.

Sometimes we might not even be aware of the loving sacrifices a friend is making on our behalf. That's what was so awesome about Jesus' sacrifice: He gave His life to save those who didn't know Him or who rejected Him as their friend.

Sacrifice for a friend is always worth it, even if it's never acknowledged, appreciated, or known. No sacrifice is ever unnoticed. Be assured that Jesus, our example, sees the sacrifices you make for your friends and will reward you in the end.

*I*f you really love one another, you will not be able to avoid making sacrifices.

Mother Teresa

*C*oncern for her friend's pain
trumped Lauren's own.
She felt powerless to change anything.

Best-Dressed Friends

Lauren looked out at the bright spring day, opened the window of her van, and let the fresh warm air rush over her. She had looked forward to this day for nearly two months. At times she had found herself smiling in anticipation of unveiling the secret she had planned for her best friend. She glanced back at the mysteriously cloaked item hanging from the hook over the backseat. Rosemary and her husband, Randall, were renewing their vows today. It was a delicious opportunity to repay the kindness Rosemary had shown

Lauren nearly twenty years before. As she drove, Lauren's mind went back to the day of their junior prom—an event that had sealed their loyalty and expressed their love for each other.

Two local high school boys had captured their hearts and asked them to the prom. Rosemary's date was Randall Beasley, her steady for almost a year and a half. For them, this prom held special significance because the following month, Randall was going to the West Coast to join the marines. It was their last high school event together; then he would be gone for two years.

Lauren's date was Tyler Cross. They had met while working on a school play three weeks earlier. Lauren was sure it was true love. Tyler was graduating but staying in the area to attend college. This would be their first big event together, and Lauren was looking forward to every moment.

The girls shopped together to find their dream dresses for the prom. Rosemary chose a hot pink, fitted dress—strapless and covered with sequins. Lauren chose a yellow chiffon, Cinderella-style gown with a sweet satin choker.

They convinced the boys that they should go as a foursome, and for the next two weeks, they spared nothing as they planned to make this the most meaningful night of their lives.

The morning of the prom, Lauren and Rosemary had their hair done at an upscale beauty shop downtown, then spent the afternoon giving each other manicures. They giggled and chatted incessantly about the evening.

They indulged in hours of primping: putting on makeup, perfume, lotions, and hair ornaments. The climax of the afternoon was the moment when they slipped into their dresses and stood before the full-length mirror. They were stunning. They admired themselves and agreed that glamour suited them well.

When the boys arrived and Rosemary's mother went to open the door, the girls ran to the top of the stairs and began their descent with an air of practiced sophistication. They had rehearsed their entry several times throughout the day because they felt clumsy in their heels and wanted to get it just right.

Chapter Five: *sacrifice*

Suddenly Lauren's heel caught in the hem of her dress. She grabbed the rail in a desperate attempt to keep from falling. But a nail sticking out from one of the vertical posts snagged her dress. It ripped a jagged tear from her knee all the way to her hem as she stumbled down two steps before catching herself. The girls gasped. The yellow chiffon was beyond repair. She couldn't possibly go to the prom with her dress in this condition.

Recognizing Lauren's grief, Tyler tried his best to comfort her. He suggested they both change clothes and go somewhere nice to eat. But his words were met by muffled sobs. Tears filled Lauren's eyes. She felt her whole evening falling apart. The four sat down on the stairs. They were silent, except for Lauren's quiet sobbing.

"You know, Tyler is right," Rosemary finally said with more cheeriness than anyone felt. "It's just a silly old prom. We don't need it to have a good time or make good memories. Let's all change and go out to dinner."

"No," Lauren protested. "You're going to the prom, and that's all there is to it. I know what this means to you with

Randall going away next month. It's the end of an era. You can't stay home on my account."

Rosemary smiled at her and said, "OK, we'll go. I'd want you to go if something happened to me. Will you at least walk me to the car?"

"Sure," Lauren said, sniffling and wiping tears from her cheeks with the back of her hand.

Rosemary took one step down the stairs, and her heel gave way. "My ankle!" she screamed. "I think I broke it!"

Lauren grabbed her arm, incredulous that this could really be happening. "What can I do? Tell me what to do," she insisted.

"Help me up," Rosemary whimpered. "I don't know if I can walk."

When she tried to stand, her ankle gave out completely, and Rosemary collapsed back onto the step. "I can't walk. I can barely get up." Rosemary began to cry softly. "Lauren, could you and Tyler please get me an ice pack from the freezer? Randall, would you carry me to my bedroom?"

Concern for her friend's pain trumped Lauren's own. She

felt powerless to change anything and so was grateful for even this small assignment to help.

As Lauren and Tyler retrieved the ice pack, she couldn't help trying to figure out what he was thinking. She didn't imagine he'd ever ask her out again after all the troubles he'd seen tonight. Lauren pushed the sadness from her mind and focused on Rosemary.

They hurried back and ran into Randall at the top of the stairs. "I think it's just a sprain," he told Lauren, "but she's in a lot of pain. She could use that ice pack right now."

Lauren rushed to Rosemary's side. "Listen," Rosemary told her. "I want you to wear my dress and go to the prom. There's no reason for both of us to miss it."

"No," Lauren objected. "I'll stay with you."

"Randall and I decided that we'd rather be alone tonight, since he's leaving so soon. It's settled, Lauren. You and Tyler are just starting out. Randall and I are old hands at this. We have last year's prom to remember." Rosemary's tone was firm. "I won't take no for an answer."

When the switch had been made, Rosemary teased affectionately as she admired Lauren in her dress. "If you were a real friend, you'd never consent to looking better in my dress than I did!"

The girls giggled, but Lauren grew somber. "I don't like this."

Rosemary squeezed her hand. "You go have fun for both of us tonight. I mean that. If you come back telling me you were miserable, you'll ruin it for both of us. Now get out of here. I want every detail when you get home."

Lauren did precisely what Rosemary asked and had the time of her life at the prom. Just before midnight, Lauren had Tyler drop her off at Rosemary's house unannounced. Through the picture window, Lauren saw Rosemary and Randall dancing. Rosemary's limp had mysteriously disappeared, and judging by her graceful movement, she was in no pain.

Lauren's face flushed hot with a sudden realization. She was tempted to barge in and scold her friend for tricking her.

But that would ruin the evening for everyone, she decided. Rosemary's was an act of devotion, and she would keep the secret until she found the perfect way to pay her back.

That day finally arrived—twenty years later.

Lauren pulled up to Rosemary's house. Chairs for the big event were set up under a large white tent in the yard. Rosemary turned to greet her. She was wearing a plain cotton dress with summer sandals and a wide-brimmed hat. Lauren knew Rosemary had wanted to buy a special gown for the ceremony, but times had been tough recently, and she wouldn't even hint of it to Randall.

Rosemary was radiant with joy. "Where's the family?" she asked.

"Oh, they'll be here soon, but I wanted to come early. I have a secret to share with you." Lauren reached inside her van and pulled out her surprise. She removed the plastic cover to reveal a beautiful, white satin wedding dress—the one she had worn to marry Tyler fifteen years ago. Rosemary gasped, speechless.

Lauren draped the dress across Rosemary's arms. "Nearly twenty years ago," she explained, "you faked an injury to trick me into wearing your dress to the prom. You gave me memories to last a lifetime. Now I'm giving you my most special dress—along with some plane tickets for a weekend in Chicago—to help you celebrate a lifetime of memories."

Rosemary buried her face in Lauren's shoulder and wept tears of joy. Lauren scolded her affectionately for smudging her makeup with sentimentality. As Rosemary retreated eagerly to put on the gown, Lauren reminded her: "If you're a real friend, you'll never consent to looking better in my dress than I did!" Rosemary turned to hug her. Lauren squeezed her friend tightly. "Now get out of here," she told her. "I'll want every detail when you get home."

Chapter Six

Dependability

the trait of being
dependable or reliable

I've planned and *know*
all of your days.
My eyes *search* the earth
to strengthen you when your *heart*
is fully *devoted* to Me.

Even if your body or your
emotions break down,
you'll have peace knowing that
I am the strength
of your heart and
your *destiny* forever!

You, in turn, demonstrate
My greatest *love*
when you sacrifice your life
for your *friends*.

KEEPING MY COVENANT OF LOVE WITH YOU,

Your Ever Present God

—from Psalms 139:16; 73:26; John 15:13; Deuteronomy 7:9

Whenever your friends mention you, it's in connection with these five words: I can always depend on… And with good reason.

Truer words could not be spoken. You're the first to arrive and the last to leave, the first to give and the last to take. When crisis comes to a friend's life, it's your name that immediately comes to mind as someone on whom a person in need can call. You always seem to know what to do, even in the worst of circumstances. When faced with hard questions, your friends know that either you'll have the answer or you'll search until you find it. If a battle is raging, you will bring peace. If someone's heart aches, you will bring healing.

inspirational message

You live like the one who said, "*Come to me, all you who are weary and burdened, and I will give you rest*" (Matthew 11:28). But Jesus didn't always wait for those in need to come to Him. Sometimes, He went to them. When His friend Thomas was confused and doubting, Jesus went to him. When the women who were His friends were grieving, He went to them. Jesus' friends learned that they could depend on Him.

Like Jesus, when others won't—or can't—come to you, you go to them. Many lives have been blessed by your help in times of need. And those who call themselves your friends know: They can always depend on you.

Friends are God's hands
extended to help.
They find joy, freely going
the extra mile to
help a friend in need…
just because they care.

LeAnn Weiss

Beth tried to scream, but the man clamped his hand over her mouth to muffle the sound.

The Winning Team

Lori and Beth's friendship had come easily. It had its beginning on a snowy November day in Colorado Springs when they were both just entering junior high. Beth was tall, athletic, and sweet-natured. Lori was petite and a bit sassy, with little interest in athletics. They had few things in common aside from their shoulder-length, sandy blond hair and expressive smiles—and a healthy sense of determination.

The girls had been paired together in gym class for a two-on-two basketball competition. Their opponents were the class snob, Heidi Hostettler, and her best friend, Susan Blake—both excellent players. Heidi was Lori's social nemesis, and Lori hated losing to her and her partner. Heidi and Susan were hardly graceful winners, and they could be obnoxious during the games.

Beth had only recently relocated and joined the school, and no one had seen her play; but all assumed from her soft appearance that she would be the weakest link in this match. "Easy win here, Susan," Heidi said to her teammate loud enough for Lori and Beth to hear.

Beth immediately sensed the tension between the girls, leaned over to Lori, and said, "Hey, you want to beat these girls?"

"Yeah, more than anything, but they're too good," Lori lamented.

"Well, I'm not a bad ball player. You get me the ball inside. We can beat this team—together." Beth's assured manner was inspiring and contagious, and the girls set out to win.

Within minutes it was clear that Lori was teamed with

one of the best basketball players in the school, and during the time they played, Beth even made Lori look like a star. The two former snobs hung their heads as they walked away with beaten egos at the short end of a 20 to 6 score. Lori and Beth had clinched both a victory and a friendship.

Throughout high school and college the girls were inseparable, their close friendship almost making them seem like one person instead of two. They called each other's parents Mom and Dad, and the two were rarely seen apart. They double-dated on most occasions and fell in love with another pair of best friends, Donny and Pat. But the most characteristic sign of their friendship was that somehow, as though they could read each other's minds, Lori and Beth always were there for each other.

It was during their senior of year of college that Beth was walking across campus to meet Lori and cut through an area called Christy Woods. She had taken that path a hundred times, but never this late at night. About halfway through the woods, she sensed danger, but she tried to calm herself by rationalizing that she was probably imagining things. Suddenly a figure leaped from behind some trees and attacked her. She tried to scream, but the man clamped his hand over her mouth to muffle the sound. All kinds of frightening thoughts raced through her mind as she tried to fight off her assailant.

Then, without warning and right beside her, Beth heard a familiar voice: "Hey, creep, chew on this for a while!" With a swift, solid crack, a heavy limb was swung with great force against the dark figure. Lori had come up behind the attacker and landed a blow so hard it sent him sprawling and then running away.

In hysterical relief, Beth lunged at Lori and hugged her so tightly she nearly shut off circulation in Lori's arms. "How did you know, Lori? How did you know I was out here in trouble?" Beth asked between sobs.

"I'm not sure, Beth—I just had a feeling, and I'm glad I followed my hunch! I love you, girl, and I don't want anything bad to happen to you."

Beth couldn't help but break into tearful laughter. "You really scared him off!"

"Hey, we can beat anything—together," Lori smiled. The two friends hugged again, then Lori escorted Beth to the police station to report the incident.

After college, Beth married Donny and moved to Seattle, Washington, where they had three boys and Donny built a career with Boeing. Lori married Pat, moved to Nashville, and had two girls and a boy while Pat built his career in the country-music industry. Though Beth and Lori stayed in touch at first, time and distance eventually had their way, and the two friends fell out of communication.

Several years later, Lori was driving home on a hot summer day when a truck crossed the centerline of the highway and forced her car off the road and into a tree at sixty miles per hour. Her legs were crushed, and she suffered a collapsed lung and several other serious internal injuries. She was rushed to the hospital, but within twenty-four hours, her kidneys started shutting down.

A doctor explained that Lori would need a kidney transplant and then delivered the grim news that the waiting list was nearly two years long. The hospital staff would try to keep her system functioning through dialysis until a matching donor organ could be found.

But Lori's condition worsened overnight, and she awoke the next morning to a roomful of bustling nurses that seemed to be preparing her for something. But through her confusion and growing panic, Lori heard a familiar voice. "Hey, you want to beat this thing?" Beth came into her line of vision, wearing the same indomitable smile she had worn when she took on the challenge of that first basketball game.

"Yeah, more than anything," Lori responded with tears and the mixed emotions of joy in the reunion and fear of the future. "But I think it's bigger than both of us."

"Well, I've got a pretty good kidney here that the doctor says will fit you perfectly," Beth answered in her familiar, assured manner. "And once you get that, I think we stand a chance." She squeezed her friend's hand with affection.

Lori was amazed at her friend's willingness to share a kidney—and at her timing. "But how did you know I was in trouble? Did Pat call you?"

"No, I just woke up yesterday and sensed that you needed me, so I called. Pat filled me in on what had happened. I caught the next flight to Nashville, and I'm glad I did! I love you, girl, and I don't want anything bad to happen to you." Beth was teary-eyed now too and hugged her friend gently. "We beat the class snobs, we beat the attacker in the woods, and we'll beat this too—together."

Chapter Seven

Faithfulness

the quality of adhering firmly and devotedly, as to a person, cause, or idea; loyalty

Know that I **never** stop *guarding* you and *tenderly* **watching** over *you.*

I command My **angels** concerning your *protection.* I'll **never** leave or *give up* on you.

Even when **you** are faithless, **you** can *count* on My **steadfast** commitment.

My love for you **endures** forever, and My *faithfulness* **continues** through all *generations.*

God of Refuge

FOREVER FAITHFUL,

Your God of Refuge

—from Psalms 121:8; 91:11; Joshua 1:5; 2 Timothy 2:13; Psalm 100:5

Faithfulness is a hallmark of friendship. It takes many forms, but perhaps the most treasured faithfulness in friendship is silence. Not a lack of communication but a communication without words. In friendship, there are times when words don't need to be spoken because friends know each other. They hear heart cries as audibly as vocal ones. And, even when a need is unspoken, they faithfully respond.

Many things can mute our cries for help, support, or encouragement. Shame, regret, and fear are silencers. Yet true friends respond faithfully, enabled by special sensors that are alerted at the smallest telltale sign of need. If someone is missing without reason, a friend starts searching. If someone is sad or weighed down by circumstances, a friend will faithfully come alongside to help lift the load. If someone fails, a friend faithfully forgives—whether or not a confession is offered.

Pain—even unexpressed pain—is felt and shared by faithful friends. They understand unspoken fears and offer assurance. Friends can sense the storms of suffering that ravage your heart, and they offer shelter. True friends faithfully fulfill the needs that go undetectable by most. Friends rush to your side without a syllable being uttered.

Friends talk about their thoughts, feelings, dreams, fears, and needs. They share laughter and tears. But the best friends are the ones who, through years of faithfulness, know us well enough to understand and respond even when we're quiet.

A faithful friend

is a strong defense;

and he that hath found him

hath found a treasure.

Louisa May Alcott

Jesse wouldn't have moved on to another location without notifying them—something had to be terribly wrong.

The Friendship Adventure

The three friends met at Woodstock in 1969. Seth, lean and tan with shoulder-length blond hair, had come for the music. Rebecca, tall and fine-featured with brunette hair and a model's sense of fashion, had come for the excitement of being at a historical event. Jesse, a southern wit who wore a baseball cap to cover his receding hairline, hitchhiked from Indiana to satisfy his hunger for adventure.

Bone weary, hungry, and thirsty, this unlikely trio met on the second night of the concert at a campsite far enough from the music to allow for conversation. After sharing the small amounts of food they had brought, they began to share their dreams, disappointments, and discoveries in life. When they learned that they lived only a short distance from each other in Indiana, the small group decided to share a bus ride home and to stay in close contact after that. As darkness fell over the camp, the light of friendship dawned in their hearts, and they became devoted soul mates.

Shortly after Woodstock, the three friends began meeting each weekend at Seth's apartment just north of Indianapolis. From there they would launch out on two-day adventures they took turns planning. When it was Seth's turn to schedule the events, the weekend was always filled with music. Often the trio attended concerts, cooked out to the sounds of their favorite artists, or went to out-of-the-way coffeehouses to hear the songs of some unknown artist.

Rebecca's weekends were wild, fast paced, and event driven: the Indianapolis 500, Fan Fair in Nashville, state fairs all over the country. Rebecca seemed to have a sense for where excitement could be found or where history was being made, and she knew how to get there.

When it was Jesse's turn at the wheel of leadership, he never ceased to amaze the other two with adventures into what he called God's sculptures on earth. The group would hike into wooded country, climbing to the top of secluded summits. Jesse's favorite weekends consisted of camping trips into the Smoky Mountains, where the three marveled at the surrounding nature and wildlife.

One particular trip into the Smokies stood out as one of their most exciting. They had started with a hike to the Chimneys, a high summit upon which stood three natural towers that offered a magnificent view of the vast mountain range. Then the three friends moved deeper into the forest to enjoy some of the most magnificent and secluded waterfalls in the park. They even ventured into some innocent but dangerous play with some bear cubs while their mother watched cautiously from a distance. This interaction with nature left them misty-eyed when it came time to return to "normal" life.

Seth, Rebecca, and Jesse developed a bond that made them more like siblings than mere friends. They were there for each other in the good times and the bad. When Rebecca's widowed mother passed away, Seth and Jesse came to help with the funeral arrangements and to stand with Rebecca as friends and neighbors filed by to pay their respects.

When Seth lost his job and was unemployed for a couple of months, Jesse and Rebecca picked up his rent and helped pay for food and utilities. After landing a good job, when Seth tried to repay them, Rebecca and Jesse refused. "Oh, we'll get the money back someday when we're in trouble, believe us. We won't forget," they insisted. But Seth knew they would.

Jesse was the only one who seemed to escape real trouble. That is, until the spring of 1973. On a rare week-end when the threesome couldn't divest themselves of other commitments, Jesse decided to take a solo trip to the Smokies. He was going through some soul searching and felt sure he would find answers in the seclusion of the mountains. He called Seth and Rebecca to let them know he was going, then set off on his excursion on Friday night.

On Sunday night, when Jesse should have returned home and normally would check in with his friends, Seth and Rebecca thought it was odd not to hear from him. They sensed that something was wrong, so they both arranged to take time off from work and headed for Tennessee. When they arrived they immediately notified the authorities. The two friends had to work to convince the rangers that Jesse wouldn't have just moved on to another location or extended his trip without notifying them—that something had to be terribly wrong.

After a series of phone calls confirming with Jesse's family that he had not been in contact with them either, search-and-rescue teams were organized and sent out. The forest service launched a massive effort, but no one could find Jesse. Days went by. Seth and Rebecca were exhausted from covering the rough terrain, and by Thursday evening authorities decided to call off the three-hundred-member search party. The nights had been unusually frigid, even for that high elevation, and experts felt certain it was too late. All hope that Jesse was alive somewhere in those mountains was gone…except for the hope in Seth and Rebecca's hearts.

The two friends were determined not to leave Jesse behind, alone in the woods—no matter what. They went into an outfitter in Knoxville and bought all the equipment they would need for an independent search. At first light on Friday morning, the pair stood at the base of the mountains and paused for a moment of prayer for their friend and for their rescue efforts. Then they set off toward the Chimneys. That was Jesse's favorite spot, and though they had covered that area before, they felt sure that would be the place they'd find Jesse.

Seth and Rebecca searched until dark, shouting Jesse's name every few feet until they were hoarse, hoping against hope that they would hear some response. Nothing. They spent that night around a campfire, alternately dozing and praying silently, and always listening for Jesse's voice.

Saturday was more of the same. More walking, more calling out, more silence. That night the two friends momentarily considered giving up. But they knew Jesse would never give up if it were them, and they determined that they wouldn't give up either.

Late Sunday evening, just when Seth and Rebecca were about to head back into town for fresh supplies, they heard a faint voice. Immediately they knew it was Jesse. Weariness replaced by adrenaline, they moved swiftly in the direction of the distant cry and kept calling out to Jesse, telling him to keep calling their names—they were coming. Within a few minutes, they came upon a wounded, bleeding, and nearly lifeless Jesse. They could see immediately that he had been mauled by a bear. He had somehow managed to drag himself to a shallow cave to take cover and await rescue.

Seth and Rebecca dropped to their knees and wrapped their arms around Jesse in grateful reunion and relieved sobs, thanking God that they had, at last, found their friend alive. Then they worked quickly to bandage Jesse's wounds and get liquid and nourishment into his dehydrated body.

Finally safe in the hands of his trusted friends, Jesse allowed tears to flow freely. He was so weak from his ordeal that he could barely speak, but Jesse motioned for Seth and Rebecca to come close. With a strained whisper Jesse spoke to his friends, pronouncing each word slowly and deliberately: "I knew you'd never give up until you found me. Thank you, friends. I love you both."